SOUL
FOOD
LOVE

SOUL
FOOD
LOVE

HEALTHY RECIPES INSPIRED by
ONE HUNDRED YEARS of COOKING
in a BLACK FAMILY

Alice Randall & Caroline Randall Williams

Photographs by Penny De Los Santos

Clarkson Potter/Publishers
New York

Copyright © 2015 by Alice Randall and Caroline Randall Williams
Principal photographs by Penny De Los Santos,
copyright © 2015 by Penny De Los Santos

Published in the United States by Clarkson Potter/Publishers, an imprint of the Crown
Publishing Group, a division of Random House LLC,
a Penguin Random House Company, New York.
www.crownpublishing.com
www.clarksonpotter.com

CLARKSON POTTER is a trademark and POTTER with colophon is a registered
trademark of Random House LLC.

"George Washington Carver Vermont Olives" first appeared in the Carver Bulletins
(August 1936). Reprinted here courtesy of Tuskegee University Archives.

Archival photographs courtesy of the author.
Photograph of Joan Williams on page 39 is reprinted courtesy of the Nashville Public Library.

Pear and carrot illustrations courtesy of Hatch Show Print®; other illustrations carved by
Bethany Taylor specifically for this book and are used with permission of the artist. Hatch
Show Print® is owned by the Country Music Hall of Fame® and Museum and operated
by the Country Music Foundation, Inc., a Section 501(c)(3) not-for-profit educational
organization chartered by the state of Tennessee in 1964.

Library of Congress Cataloging-in-Publication Data
Randall, Alice.
Soul food love : healthy recipes inspired by one hundred years of cooking
in a black family / Alice Randall and Caroline
Randall Williams ; photographs by Penny De Los Santos.
Includes index.
1. African American cooking. I. Williams, Caroline Randall. II. Title.
TX715.R2136 2015
641.59'296073—dc23   2014014423

ISBN 978-0-804-13793-5
eBook ISBN 978-0-804-13794-2

Printed in China

Book design by La Tricia Watford
Cover design by La Tricia Watford and Gabriel Levine
Cover photographs by Penny De Los Santos
Cover illustrations courtesy of Hatch Show Print®;
eggplant and bell pepper by Bethany Taylor

10 9 8 7 6 5 4 3 2 1

First Edition

TO MIMI,
WHOSE SOUL, FOOD, AND LOVE
HAVE SUSTAINED US
FOR SO LONG

CONTENTS

Preface

A TALE OF FIVE KITCHENS

This cookbook tells the story of five kitchens—three generations of women who came to weighing more than two hundred pounds, and a fourth generation that absolutely refused ever to weigh two hundred pounds. It's the story of a hundred years of cooking and eating in one black American family.

On these pages we share the kitchen memories, kitchen gossip, and foodways that sustained two great-grandmothers, a grandmother, and us: a mother and a daughter.

Dear's kitchen, Grandma's kitchen, Nana's kitchen, Mama's kitchen (Alice's), and Baby Girl's kitchen (Caroline's). All are sacred places in our family. But only one is simple: Baby Girl's.

The recipes in this book are from Baby Girl's kitchen. You can cook every one from a Walmart shelf. Or you can cook them from your home garden, or Whole Foods—but wherever you get your foodstuffs, cook these recipes and you will be tasting the past swerving into a new and healthier future. You will be tasting us using what we got to get where we want to go—to Fitland without forgetting, shaming, or blaming traditional soul foods or traditional soul foodways.

Our kitchen celebrates forgotten soul food staples. We love sweet potatoes, peanuts, and sardines. Our ancestresses loved them, too. For us the path to our black food future runs through our black food past. And it requires radical change.

The kitchen has historically been a fraught place for many black Americans. Our family is among the many. It has been a place of servitude and scarcity, and sometimes violence, as well as a place of solace, shelter, creativity, commerce, and communion.

In our family, and in many Southern families, the abundant kitchen has become an antidote for what pains and afflicts us. Somewhere along the way, abundance became excess. Then the excess became illness.

Today the kitchen that once saved us is killing us. And avoidance of the kitchen is killing us, too. Foodways in much of black America are plain broke-down. Too many young black women have lower life expectancies than their mothers. And most don't even know it.

And it's not just black America. The Sun Belt is now the Stroke Belt. Fat-fueled diseases—diabetes, hypertension, stroke, and cancer—ravage the nation. But black America is particularly hard hit.

We can change that in the kitchen, on the quick and on the cheap. We know because we did it in our family—fought back hard against fat while holding proud to our table. Others are doing it, too, becoming kitchen-sink Amazons—winning the war on fat—one tasty home-fixed and healthy meal at a time.

And by home-fixed we're not talking just about where you cook. We're talking about *what* you cook. We're talking about connecting with our mothers' mothers through taste. We're talking about celebrating all we created and all we endured by holding close to some of the flavors that were with us when we were creating and enduring.

And we're talking about letting some of them go. Anything that's killing us is poison, not food.

The kitchens in this book are the kitchens that had the most impact on our bodies and lives. As with many black families, there are missing leaves in our family tree. Alice's mother, who never cooked for Caroline and seldom cooked for Alice, was orphaned at five. The Lutheran Lady, as she styled herself, didn't know either of her grandmothers and barely remembered her mother. We think they were from Ohio. Those leaves remain lost.

But there are leaves aplenty. And they are scattered widely.

Kitchens, like people, migrate. The kitchens we will recollect were located, at various times, in three different Southern states—Georgia, Alabama, and Tennessee; in the Midwestern metropolises of Detroit and Chicago; and in the imperial black city of the East Coast: Harlem.

Some of the kitchens that go into the making of our tables were constructed in dire poverty, others in sepia privilege. All of this allows us to claim: if you're a black American, our roots are likely to cross yours. We cover a lot of territory.

Tracing kitchen migrations, we've encountered many surprises.

A pleasant one we found while shaking our culinary family tree: one of the earliest black vegan movements—the black Seventh-day Adventists. Grandma spent a good part of her life as an Adventist cooking vegetarian recipes supplied by *The Message,* a black Seventh-day Adventist magazine.

All the surprises were not pleasant. Until we started working together on this volume, we knew the kitchen was a difficult territory for some black women, but we had never contemplated the significance of kitchen rape—an event we discovered was sufficiently common in our family history as to merit the coining of a phrase so the atrocity might be better mourned.

Dear was born in the nineteenth century, 1897. Baby Girl was born in the twentieth century, 1987, and came of age in the twenty-first. The family kitchen stories we have collected stretch across three centuries. We are proud to write that. Within Dear's and Grandma's stories are accounts they heard directly from aunts and grandmothers who were enslaved. These are the tales and recipes of generations learning and re-learning to feed themselves, their families, and their communities in adversity and prosperity, in rural acres and on urban corners in America.

Our ideal is a table that delights, fortifies, and remembers.

The recipes are the work of a daughter who searched out the healthier bites and bits from her family's cooking history and remixed the best of the rest into something greener, into something healthier and easier— working beside a mother determined to change her own foodways so she might change her daughter's food future. This is the story of our search for a kitchen where what's good is good for you.

And nothing is finer than a good taste on a healthy tongue.

Dear

MINNIE RANDALL

(1897-1976)

Minnie rarely cooked. She appeared to cook. Daily. Her husband, Will Randall, who had grown up in Selma, Alabama, around white women who never lifted a hand in their own kitchens, couldn't stand to see his Negro wife peel a potato or quarter a hen.

So Will did all the peeling and chopping, the snapping of beans and cleaning of greens, the mixing and stirring. Dear finished the food and served it. First in Selma, then in Detroit.

In Detroit on Sunday it was hen simmered in one pot, beef rump roasted with turnips and carrots in the other pot. Always two choices of meat on the Sabbath. Served alongside: a pan of cornbread dressing that looked like a sheet cake, or a bowl of whole-kernel hominy.

Friday supper was always fish, usually pan-fried lake perch. Or it could be my father's favorite, red snapper, iced and trained or trucked up from the Gulf Coast, purchased at Giles Fish and Poultry Market the day it would be cooked; dusted with salt, pepper, and paprika; then baked.

Every morning there was hot breakfast, typically skillet cornbread made with yellow cornmeal, flour, and bacon drippings or maybe hoecakes made with just yellow cornmeal.

Six of the seven days a week he cooked, Will moved stealthily between his home in the Black Bottom neighborhood of old Detroit and the thriving dry cleaners he and his wife proudly co-owned and co-ran next door. But he allowed Mrs. Randall to claim the food.

Hot dinner at noon, supper come dark. Every day.

Sometimes on days when business in the dry cleaning shop was exceptionally good and they were exceptionally busy (at the counter, at the presses, at the cleaning machines, at the sewing machines), my grandfather would be slammed at the cash register, overseeing. Those days Paw Paw would slip almost invisibly inside Dear's kitchen, peel and slice mounds and pounds of sweet potatoes and onions, and set them to slow sautéing in a pan before moving back to his visible perch behind the counter in his shop.

Sweet potato hash and other reliable sustenance—for growing boys and girls who ripened into working men and women, for the entrepreneurial brood that became their dazzling family, four tall boys and two stylish daughters—was always provided at Dear's house.

Eventually Minnie and Will retired from the cleaners to a three-bedroom brick home with lush ferns lining the steps and balustrade of the spacious porch out front, hundreds of rosebushes, and a goldfish pond out back. The trim bride of her wedding photographs was now a matron with a mink coat and a closet full of size 24 dresses. No longer busy in the shop, bookkeeping or subbing as counter girl or performing alterations, Minnie became an ambitious, able, and ardent grandmother, gardener, and confectionaire.

Will kept cooking.

As a child in the early '60s I knew Dear to be graceful and gracious, vivacious and loving. Paw Paw was exhausted. My father attributed Paw Paw's exhaustion to the death of Bill, Will's eldest son, in 1958.

Dear lost that boy, too, and she brought him into this world from her own body. I think Paw Paw's exhaustion had more to do with the fact that for about fifty years he worked two hard jobs. He worked for himself as a serial and successful entrepreneur, able to purchase and provide brick houses, cars, and lovely furniture for his family. And he worked as Dear's very able kitchen man.

• • •

Minnie was a girl of fifteen and Will was a man of twenty-five when they married and set up their first kitchen and home in Selma, Alabama, in 1913.

Around the time Dear was sitting in her first married-lady kitchen, there was a lynching of a black person by the name of Carson in Selma. Two years later a black woman, Hope Hull, would be lynched down the road in Birmingham.

These were events that would be chewed over at the Randall family table as my grandparents started making babies and plans for a bigger and safer life than what was typically available to colored folk in Dallas County, Alabama, in the early days of the twentieth century.

Even for a man industrious enough to arrange to buy used clothes up north in Chicago and have them transported south, where the clothes were cleaned and mended and resold at prices below new—but still at a profit—a man sufficiently prideful and prosperous to be always wearing a suit and a tie whenever seen outside the house, even for such a man as

Will and Minnie Randall,
Alabama, circa 1913.

that, when the man was black, and his wife was black, Selma was no safe or simple place.

One of Dear and Paw Paw's strategies for providing a sense of emotional security and resilience for themselves and for their offspring was to create a culture of abundance and a culture of difference, rooted in the kitchen.

Starting at, and by, the stove, they did not abide by the normal rules. Will worked outside the home and Will worked inside the home.

Freed from the challenge of providing daily meals, Dear turned her attention, both in Alabama and later in Michigan, to the task of educating their children.

Compounding the common challenges black parents faced in the segregated school systems of the Jim Crow era was Dear and Paw Paw's unwillingness to send their children to public school in Alabama because they believed "they beat the colored kids so bad."

Despite the fact Dear was barely literate, her husband was illiterate, and the law did not allow it, Dear homeschooled in Selma, and she did most of it in her kitchen and at her lace-covered dining table.

She had an ally: the black church. She kept her children's butts in the pews, not searching for God but seeking the rich introduction to rhetoric, reasoning, and rhyme that could be found in the sermons. She taught her sons and daughters to read by liberal application of the King James Bible. When they arrived in Michigan she was as insistent that her children's butts be in school chairs when the school doors were open as she had been about church, which for the children became optional.

Once my father boasted to me, when I first read *Macbeth* at my fancy private school, that he had memorized a whole Shakespeare play—I believe he said it was *King Lear*—before graduating from high school. I asked him how he could do that when he had barely gone to grade school before enrolling at Miller High. He responded simply, "Shakespeare's not that different from the Bible."

While Dear focused her kitchen energies on education, Paw Paw kept cooking—and scheming to build an empire. His plans found the family relocated to Detroit in about 1941.

The plan worked. Eventually two sons established thriving dry cleaners of their own. One daughter owned a small apartment building and a tiny fleet of cabs. The other daughter owned a corner store licensed to sell liquor. Everybody had a pocketful of money and a house of their own, and everyone ate out in the streets.

Yes, Dear's sons and daughters' faces and figures were well known in the nightclubs, show bars, supper clubs, and blind pigs of Paradise Valley and larger Motown. If the Top of the Flame and the Driftwood Lounge beckoned them in, so did, eventually, the long-segregated Pontchartrain and the London Chop House as barriers fell and Randall wealth increased.

By the time I was born, in 1959, my father and his siblings did not sit down to eat hot "dinner" cooked on a home stove at midday. Instead they grabbed lunch on the go from a barbecue joint, or Coney Island (diners specializing in a Detroit delicacy, a beef hot dog in a natural casing slathered with a particular commercially made beef chili), or a sub shop, or, best yet in my daddy's calculations, pulled out of a vending machine in his own dry cleaners.

But Dear's children did not stay out in the streets on the seventh day. The most important meal of every week was quiet and private: dinner at Dear's on Sunday.

Minnie Randall holding
her firstborn son,
Bill, circa 1917.

Dear's kitchen was the magnet home.

When the children were grown, each of them had a key to the house and an invitation to come eat on Sunday at the hour of their choosing. The Sunday dinner was waiting on the stove any time you looked for it after noon. Chicken in one pot. Beef in the other. And there was always enough for grandbabies and in-laws.

The adult Randall siblings in the '60s did not go to church on Sunday. They went to Dear's. As a toddling cousin stated and adults in the family frequently repeated: Dear's house got every stuff!

On Hazelwood "every stuff" was a righting of previous privations. It was intimate yet also political.

Intimate abundance: the lush largeness of Dear's lap, the vast pillow-softness of her huge upper arms, and best, Dear's immense bosom, always modestly covered with a bodice of a pretty cotton or silk.

We all knew, even the children, what stuff was found in abundance at Dear's. First and foremost, Dear's ripe and huge body. But also: good talk, good love, good money, and great food.

My grandparents had reconstructed a dynamic of the old South. Dear claimed, and was lauded for, a table she did not create. Now typically this was white women claiming the work of black women without their free consent. In Dear's case it was a woman claiming the work of a man—with his free consent.

And so it came to be that Dear was allowed an eminence in the domestic sphere without being shackled to the kitchen.

I've always known that my father's family, when it came to the kitchen, was what the old black folk called "different." When I was a young girl staying overnight with Dear and Paw on Hazelwood, Paw Paw cooked me cornbread baked in a cast-iron skillet and brewed fresh coffee on an open gas flame. It was Paw Paw who sat with me at the kitchen table to eat.

Dear sat me down at the table in her dining room, the most formal room in the house, to read. The large and fancy wooden table was typically spread with a hand-crocheted cloth. She would sit me up in one of the high-backed copies of a Chippendale chair and serve up a book. When I was finished with one, she would present me with another. Two or three times a day I got to sit at the table and she served up books like other grandmas served up bacon and bread.

On the occasions Dear worked alone in the kitchen on a dish from start to finish, it would be on something quietly extravagant. Crustless sandwiches cut into charming shapes. Ice cubes with fruit frozen into them. Candied apples with the dense, sugary texture of marrons glacés, dyed bright blue or green, that we called dress-box apples.

I loved her dress-box apples. To this day they may be the most splendidly presented dish I have ever tasted. To open a gift-wrapped dress box, complete with foil paper and huge bow, and discover inside not an item of clothing but a dozen or more apples with their stems in jewel-toned blue or green or purple, was to be thrilled into believing there was a place where the real world and fairyland intersected—and that spot was in a pot on Dear's stove, in Dear's kitchen.

Dress-box apples are powerful. They confound expectation. Loudly and visually they say, "Magic is real."

When you are small and are given this lavish gift, you feel royal before you know the word. You cannot eat a dress-box apple and feel like a picka-ninny. You cannot eat a dress-box apple and believe you have not tasted some of the best this world has to offer. To bite into a dress-box apple is to wonder if you have not tasted better than every blue-eyed white-skinned girl in your picture books who wears a golden crown or slipper and is called "princess."

Dear cooked like she cured the blues from mosquito bites on hot sum-mer nights: gloriously and only for immediate black family.

When grandchildren would come to visit she would put them in the back bedroom overlooking the roses, next to the bathroom. The house on Hazelwood was not air-conditioned. In the middle of the night while the grandchildren were sleeping, she would come to our room and dab all of our mosquito bites with perfume. The alcohol would staunch the itch and the sweet smell of perfume could waft a Dear-loved child back to dreamland.

Looking back it would not be a lie to say: Dear didn't cook, she sweetened. Those dress-box apples: bushels of Michigan apples poached in sugar water and dyed eye-popping pretty. Blackberries for a crustless cobbler. Sweet potatoes weighted down with dark brown sugar and molas-ses for a pie. Sugar tits for visiting infants.

She wasn't interested in providing sustenance—she left that to her husband. She provided comfort and medicine.

Dear had a very limited medicine cabinet. It contained white sugar, Coca-Cola, aspirin, whiskey, lemon, and honey. If a child wouldn't eat breakfast or an adult felt puny, she, like many black mothers of the Great Migration, prescribed "Co-Cola" and aspirin. If you had a cough, it was equal parts honey, whiskey, and lemon. If your heart was broke, or you felt shamed, or felt unwanted, or felt unable, she gave you some form of sugar. If you were scared, you got a swig of whiskey. But most often she prescribed and dispensed sugar. As far as she knew it had the fewest complications.

She didn't know about metabolic syndrome. Didn't know that, a hundred years after she prescribed her first "Co-Cola" and aspirin, black American men, women, and children would consume disproportionately high amounts of sugary soft drinks. Didn't know we'd become obese— who had ever heard of such a word?—and have health problems that would shorten our life spans.

She knew about the relationship between food and mood. She understood she could impact the mental health of her family with sugar— because she regulated her own mental health with hourly doses of sugar. Kit Kat bars and peppermints were her drugs of choice. She reached for Russell Stover chocolates like some skinny modern mothers facing real-world-big problems reach for a Xanax. She swilled sweet tea like it was morphine. She treated pain, shame, fear, and exhaustion with the same medicine her grandmother had used to treat her pain, shame, and fear when she was a child—with sugar water.

For me the sugar tit is the saddest recipe in the soul food canon: Take a clean and unstarched white handkerchief. Drop it in a pot of simmering sugar water. With strong clean hands, wring it till it doesn't drip. Make sure the cloth is still warm. Fold the cloth and twist it into a thick coil. Hand it to a howling baby whose mama has gone—often to work. Sugar tit.

Empty, solacing, body-blighting calories.

Dear sucked sugar tits in her childhood. Both Paw Paw and Dear had white fathers who came from prominent Alabama families. After her liaison with Dear's father, Dear's mother, Betty, went on to marry a relatively prosperous black farmer and have more children, forming a strong family that Dear was connected to, but never completely a part of, and didn't live with.

I have second and third cousins who fondly remember my great-grandmother Betty Johnson's Alabama farm. They remember robust gardens: beans and greens, and tomatoes, and melon. They remember chicken and eggs from the place. And pigs. As one elderly cousin stated to me in a phone call while I was working on this cookbook, "We ate out the garden. Beets, turnip greens, collard greens, okra, 'tater salad, peppers, cabbage, watermelons, chickens, turkeys, hogs." They remember cutting sugarcane and grinding it to syrup with the help of a mule. They remembered an all-black, all-family, self-sustained farm bubble a mile from the main road and the world, where they ate from the soil and little or nothing they ate came from a store.

Dear lived in exile from that farm. She hardly knew her mother, Betty. She didn't know mother's breast milk. She knew her grandmother Nancy and sugar tits.

Dear sucked and remembered sugar tits, prepared by her grandmother in the absence of her mother. She knew sweet as an antidote to the sting of the South. Dear remembered living with her father's white family, cared for by her black grandmother, and then living alone with her black grandmother. She remembered the black farmers who sold produce to the white family and how disdainfully they were treated.

Though the farm foodstuffs her cousins recalled with pleasure were also some of the foodstuffs that would have appeared on Paw Paw and Dear's Selma table, where Paw Paw and Dear first chewed over lynchings and the possibilities and the necessity of leaving Alabama, for Dear, eating these wholesome farm foods was never an act of simple pleasure.

Minnie and Will Randall in Detroit in the 1950s.

If Dear recalled the Johnson family farm as an eye in the middle of the storm that was Jim Crow, it was an island she understood to be precarious and vulnerable. She understood what her husband, Will, understood: that every acre of the black Southern farm was fertilized with the memory of slavery, watered with the shaming of Jim Crow, seeded with the descendants of kitchen rapes during and after slavery, and tilled with the ever-present threat of lynching.

In the land of strange fruit, farm-to-table food, urban chicken coops, even cool juicy watermelon have complex resonances often overlooked, ignored, or misread.

Dear didn't overlook, ignore, or misread the complexities. She fell in love with every process that distanced food from the farm and every habit that freed her from the kitchen her black grandmother had been shackled to in her white father's home.

And so it was that Will kept cooking and Dear kept growing flowers even as the family began to eat out more and carry in more; became intrigued with TV dinners and Tang, with smorgasbords and bars, with all the fancy eats money could buy or market could imagine. Fascinated by everything that promised modernity and with it equal opportunity and safety, that came with distance from Alabama, Southern rural kitchens, and rural acres. Paw Paw and Dear associated soil food with the life they had left behind in the South. Processed food equaled progress.

I didn't learn to cook a single dish in my grandmother's kitchen.

The man who figured out how to rig a car seat with telephone books so five-year-old me could sit up to see over the wheel and steer in the cemetery, so he could teach me "to drive," didn't figure out how to hold me up to the stove to stir a pot or measure cornmeal for cornbread. He didn't want to.

Paw Paw kept me scared in the kitchen. Over and over he warned me to turn the handle of the big black frying pan inward, alerting me to be watchful and make sure no one else had left a handle turned outward. He told tales of hot grease burning feet and faces to drive home his point. Though I was barely allowed to approach the stove, I was frequently admonished to keep all dry fabric (sleeve, dishcloth, clean dishrag) away from the open flame. The only time he ever threatened me with violence, or to punish me at all, he used kitchen language and threatened to wield a kitchen object: on a drive to school I will never forget as long as I live, he told me to stop crying, get out of the car, and get in the school door or he was going to "whip me with a wet dishrag." Paw Paw did not work to make me comfortable in the kitchen—he did everything he could to make me afraid of it. Like most everything else he tried to do, he got the job done.

Grandma

ALBERTA JOHNSON BONTEMPS

(1906–2004)

G randma cooked for the chosen.

It was in the middle of her life, and in the middle of World War II, after she landed on the Fisk campus in Nashville in 1943 as the wife of Harlem Renaissance poet Arna Bontemps and sometimes muse of Langston Hughes, that Alberta Bontemps came into her full power in the kitchen: cooking for clubwomen.

In the twentieth century, Nashville was home to scads of social clubs woven intimately into the fabric of the black town. Though many, but by no means all, of these clubs are now extinct, up to and through the 1950s and '60s it was not uncommon for a person of means, popularity, and African descent to join multiple clubs. Grandma, for instance, belonged to two bridge clubs, the Vagabonds and the Iris Bridge Club; a garden club, the Ardent Gardeners; and a national club, the Links, Incorporated.

The Links. The Circle-ettes. The Boulé. The Fine Arts Club, Gaieté de Coeur Art and Study Club, the Vagabonds, the Faculty Breakfast Club, the

Twenty-One Club, the Aurora Assembly, Agra Assembly, the Nine-ettes, Un Mazzo di Carte, the Sportsman Club, Vingt-et-Un, the Gleaners Club—the list of clubs joined by black Nashvillians goes on and on, though sadly some of the names of the local, if once exquisite, clubs are starting to be forgotten.

The Links is often described as the black equivalent of the Junior League. Membership means you have achieved a nationally recognized elite social status. The Iris Bridge Club is an all-black club so exclusive that many members of the Links don't know it exists. The Iris Bridge Club once went seventeen years without being able to agree on a single new member. Then they took me. Such was Grandma's sway.

In her heyday, Alberta owned, washed, and polished forty place settings of ornate silver, stacks of matching fine china plates, and more than a hundred delicate party glasses. And she weighed over two hundred pounds.

For a big club function, say a bridge club lunch, she would set up folding card tables all through her formal living room ten days before the event. After she draped those metal tables with perfectly washed, starched, and ironed linens, she would tenderly lay them with napkins, china, silver, and glass. When her tables were just so, she covered each one with a white bedsheet she kept for the sole purpose of shielding tablescapes from dust.

She set the tables a week in advance of club meeting so that she could spend the entire week shopping, menu-refining, prep-cooking, and cooking.

Her favorite foods were bridge party food, and Links food, company's-coming food. Complex chicken salads. Elaborate aspics. Checkerboard sandwiches. Rum balls. Tall layer cakes. Home-frozen custards. Roasted turkeys. Shrimp Creole. Salmon molds. These were the dishes that established her reputation as a hostess beyond the family circle, and these were the dishes she cherished and perfected, the building blocks of her many memorable feasts for other clubwomen.

These were self-consciously important meals, designed to be as difficult for the chef as they were delightful for the guest. They were performances of taste and imagination, of relative prosperity wed to abundant good sense. They were not financially extravagant. They were decidedly not performances of the power of purchase. They were demonstrations of kitchen skill and time commitment. They were above all meant to convey via tongue but not talk, *You are worthy.*

In a Jim Crow world in which persons of African descent were daily reminded that they were not worthy—to drink out of the same drinking fountain as whites, to sit at the front of the bus or at a dime store lunch counter and drink a cup of coffee and eat a chicken sandwich—Mrs. Bontemps and other black clubwomen throughout Nashville and across the country cooked up a black bourgeois bubble where black worth was celebrated and tasted.

Executing this act of rebellion could be a daunting task.

In Nashville, as in so many segregated cities in the South between the Civil War and Vietnam, if you were black and wanted to enjoy fancy food outside your home, you had to join a club—which meant you had to turn your home into a banquet hall when it came your turn to host.

"Your turn to host!" In the black South this simple declaration has been known to bring strong women to tears, churchwomen to curses, good marriages to the brink of divorce, and to drag the financially astute out of the black ink and into red.

These women understood that they were being asked to create an occasional meal so dignified it was a cure for a myriad of daily race-based indignities. So original it defied and exploded stereotypes. So cosmopolitan it claimed a planet as theirs. They were being asked to present a meal that was no less than an act of civil realignment.

Women who never hit their children, never cursed their husbands, never dropped a friend, never bounced a check, were known to commit all four of these sins and a few more when it was their "turn."

Not Grandma. For Grandma her turn was her turn to shine.

Grandma believed identity could be painted on the tongue with flavor. She believed that her pots and her spoons could be equal to paper and pen, or canvas and pigment. She understood the club meeting meal to be an art form, and the great club meeting hostesses to be artists. And she understood her art to be political.

If some folks thought she was just an amazing housewife, she didn't set them straight. She loved to tell the story of Fisk president Charles Spurgeon Johnson (not to be confused with Mordecai Johnson at Howard) arriving unannounced at her house early on a Sunday morning to see if everything was always so perfect. He discovered it was. Not a dirty dish in the sink and hot breakfast on a cloth-covered table. Ringing round, every child in his or her chair, starched and fully dressed with a clean face and a fresh napkin in the lap. Capping it all, the scent of flowers fresh from Alberta's garden mingled with the aroma of strong coffee. Johnson took a sip. A legend was born before it was time to leave for church.

When Johnson's wife, who had been out of town when Alberta first arrived, finally met her at a party where people were already talking about Alberta's recipes and Alberta's way of doing things, Mrs. Johnson exclaimed to Alberta, "I wanted to give this party to launch you—but I see you've already been launched!"

The wall-washing stay-at-home wife and mother excelled when cooking for exacting beige, brown, and jet-black ladies in girdles and stockings and silk suits, with pearls around their necks, who wore their husband's wedding rings converted to gold pins on their shoulder when they became widows. With every morsel she cooked she understood herself to be challenging assumptions about what it means to be black. Every bite she cooked for her clubwomen said: hardworking, detail-loving, imaginative, sensualist—that is me.

As a party chef cooking for the wives of black professors, college administrators, doctors, and lawyers, Grandma Bontemps was fastidious and original.

If a thing was to be done, it was to be done exactly right. A birthday cake had at least three layers of cake, and possibly four or five! It would also have at least one filling—lemon and strawberry were favorites—that was different from the outer layer of a buttery-rich frosting that swathed the whole affair. Lemons were rinsed in warm water and rolled on a table before they were juiced. Shrimp were deveined once and inspected twice.

Even as she reveled in creating opulence on an honest brain-earned (by her husband) dollar, she charmingly honored the frugality in which her cooking, developed in the Depression era, was rooted.

Two dozen daffodils, cut with no present expense from her garden, stuck into the middle of and spraying out of the top of a giant glass urn, once she had filled it full of cheap lemons (that were later turned into lemonade) and almost free water, created an elegant celebration of the color yellow for a spring club meeting. Any time of year, hours of free child labor spent churning could turn grocery-store milk, eggs, sugar, and vanilla into frozen custards that could be further transformed, with the help of treasured copper molds, into elaborate whimsical shapes that provoked days of happy gossip and advanced her legend as the perfect clubwoman.

The first time I played bridge and ate lunch with the ladies of the Iris Bridge Club, it was at Grandma's house on Geneva Circle in a prosperous hilltop neighborhood largely populated by retired professors and administrators of three extraordinary black institutions of higher learning: Meharry Medical College, Tennessee State University, and Fisk University.

When the bridge club met at Grandma's, members arrived with perfectly done hair and played in a room decorated with large oil paintings by the man she called "Doug," whom others knew as Aaron Douglas, the foremost painter of the Harlem Renaissance. In a glass case against one living room wall were hand-typed books—Christmas gifts that Lang (Langston Hughes) had prepared for one or another of the children.

Grandma had come a long way from Du Pont, Georgia.

• • •

The story Alberta told me of her conception and childhood in Georgia centered on kitchens. She said her grandmother worked as a domestic for a prominent white family in Waycross. Eventually Alberta's grandmother took her own daughter (Alberta's mother) to work for the same family. The first day she was in the house she was raped by a son of the white family.

Much of Alberta's very early life was spent in her white grandmother's kitchen as her black grandmother cooked and cleaned the home of her own daughter's rapist.

When Grandma Bontemps told me the story, she said her mother went crazy after the rape and abandoned Alberta to be raised as an only child by her grandmother and a root-doctor aunt who had been born a slave. She said she was a chubby baby and child, a marker of relative privilege. She had enough to eat even if some of it was scraps. Others didn't even have that. Grandma didn't forget.

The stove in Grandma's first home kitchen figured significantly, but not as a source of food. It was remembered as a place to boil sassafras and blackberry root, eggshells, and iodide potash. As Grandma often told me, her aunt made her living delivering babies and curing venereal disease in the turpentine camps, where poor people, almost all black, toiled slashing cat faces into pine trees that would bleed gum to be boiled and distilled into turpentine and rosin. In Grandma's memory the home kitchen was a place for cooking up cures.

And the kitchen where food was cooked was a place where you worked for other people.

Eventually the black grandmother and aunt collaborated with Alberta to have Alberta sent to New York to go to high school. Grandma lived with a Jewish family, working as a kind of au pair, while attending a black Seventh-day Adventist high school. At Harlem Academy on West 127th Street, Alberta met and fell in love with Arna Bontemps, one of her professors. In 1926 they were married and Alberta began cooking.

When Grandma regaled me with stories of her various kitchens and various days cooking, there were six distinct eras: her golden Harlem Renaissance young-married days of oatmeal and pea soup; her Huntsville, Alabama, Oakwood College plantation nightmare where she learned to make Adventist meatloaf and other vegetarian delicacies; her Chicago sojourn where she learned to cook from cans; her Fisk campus launch and rise to dominance with the party food; the international period when she traveled with her husband to Yale and abroad, expanding her food vocabulary exponentially; and her widowhood in Nashville, cooking for clubwomen and family, eventually editing a lifetime of cooking and eating into her version of the perfect family feast.

It was always evident that the period she loved most was the Fisk period, which came after years of toiling in the kitchen to raise her family.

Mrs. Bontemps, the artist-chef-hostess, started off as kitchen drudge. She developed her considerable cooking skills putting three meals a day on the table seven days a week. In her prime, the years when she had a husband and six children at home, she cooked on average 168 plates a week, about 9,000 plates a year—including meals for visiting family and friends.

Grandma did not regularly enlist children or spouse to get basic meals on the table. She perpetuated a pattern observed in her youth—her kitchen was a space where she worked for other people. But she did achieve a significant innovation: the people she worked for were truly beloved by her. They were her blood family and dear friends, not employers.

In Nashville Grandma Bontemps entered a halcyon era. She was a matron with a capital M. For the first time she was armed with a budget, fueled by Arna's salary and Arna's copyrights, sufficient to provide a gracious plenty. And so she started cooking for the clubwomen, evolving and editing the specialties of her various houses to create a celebratory board that became self-expressive art.

I have a copy of a photograph of a Links meeting in 1962. In the photograph, Grandma, short and wide, is on the far right. Like most of the women, she's wearing a black cocktail dress. Hers features buttons—they appear to be silver—down the front. Her collar is beaded or jeweled, the sleeves are three-quarter. She's dressed to work and to play. And she's gazing back at her club sisters, not out to the camera.

There are quite a few trim women in this bunch, but there are also colossal women. Many of the colossal women were Grandma's best friends. The largest ladies appear of sufficient girth to carry the race, and what the race needed, forward in their massive hulls. The thin women seem, in this photograph and in much of Grandma's storytelling, to be traveling light, carrying no one but themselves, attracting nothing but the attention of less worthy men.

Grandma believed matriarchs grew large. And in her world they often did. Starting with Grandma.

Though the club meeting meal was Grandma's métier, her cooking was rooted in and refined by the daily toil of cooking half a million simple family meals.

But how simple were they, really? If the typical family meal of her early childhood consisted of one biological grandmother cooking as a servant for her other biological grandmother; consisted of seeing and hearing part of her family, the white part, eat in the dining room while she ate scraps, or not at all, or succulent bits held back from the white table in the dining room by her black grandmother expressly to be presented to young Alberta in the kitchen—how could the meal be simple?

And if she ate with her white father, perhaps a piece of fried chicken and a hot biscuit, could that have been a simple meal? She would have had to know the only place they could eat together was the kitchen. She might have learned that her father was her mother's rapist. And perhaps she would have learned that the assault began in the kitchen. No, the family meal was not simple, not for Alberta.

Cooking for clubwomen with all its virtuoso complexity was far simpler than cooking for family, in no small part because it was utterly new.

She loved celebrating herself and women like herself who had survived to thrive and refine. She inhabited a space of bourgeois elegance that was slyly yet profoundly radical. It makes all the difference in the world when the women doing the eating, and the women doing the cooking, serving, and cleaning, knew themselves to be equals, peers, like-minded, and like-fated.

To taste what Mrs. Bontemps served you was to know the cook was a worthy woman. In this way she and other clubwomen also honored their foremothers, who never got to sit at any formal dining room table but served.

By the time I met her in the mid-1980s, when her grandson Avon Nyanza Williams started courting me, Grandma was slowing down. She was still a size 20 but she was starting to shrink.

Her last great clubwoman hurrah was my wedding reception at the Cosmos Club in Washington, D.C. With access to a clubhouse and a chef, Grandma went to town planning. The idea for the menu was straightforward: Pain Perdu, Étouffée or Jambalaya, and Shrimp Creole. We wanted dishes that would bring the spirit of Arna Bontemps to the party. The wedding cake itself would be dessert. There would be champagne and there would be coffee. Inexpensive and elegant, our wedding feast, after the high noon church service, was a classic Alberta Bontemps perfect bridge party luncheon—without the cards.

After the reception we set off on our honeymoon. Grandma headed off to the hospital. While we were on the honeymoon, she had a double mastectomy. A hip replacement and cataract surgery followed. Eventually a hysterectomy and even hand surgery for a skin cancer. It became less and less possible for Grandma to entertain as she liked to entertain—doing all the work herself. And she buried friend after friend until it came to be that I could fit all that remained of what had once been a large and vibrant social circle of more than two hundred ladies into a single limousine that drove the group to Grandma's favorite spots around the city while they ate chicken salad sandwiches and lemon chess squares—her beloved bridge party food.

Alberta Bontemps entertaining great-granddaughter Caroline Randall Williams at her second birthday party in Nashville, 1989.

Deep into her nineties, Grandma still gave parties. And she still did some cooking. Only eventually—with the possibility of Grandma having to cancel once invitations were issued due to her ill health, and the challenges she faced when getting dressed in less than comfortable and efficient clothes—all the party guests were kin.

• • •

Other families celebrated the birth of the Christ child by setting up crèches and placing tiny dolls in toy mangers, or by acting in the Christmas pageant. Grandma baked birthday cake.

Every year on December 24 she baked and frosted a from-scratch, many-layered coconut cake, then stuck a candle in its center. On December 25, at the end of Christmas dinner, the youngest child present blew the candle out as the family sang "Happy Birthday, Baby Jesus." In Grandma-Bontemps-world, every year the Baby Jesus turned one.

A few years after I married her grandson, Avon, the child blowing out the candle was my own Caroline. While I was pregnant waiting for Caroline to be born, I lived with Grandma on Geneva Circle, often sleeping in Arna's old library. It was during this time that Grandma told me about a pre-clubwomen cooking experience that had thrilled her: making baby food for her firstborn.

Grandma boasted that Queen Elizabeth, born the same year as her eldest child, "ate no better than my Joan." Then she began to regale me with tales of peeling the skin off a hundred *individual* peas to make a single delicious meal for her Joan. Cheap but exquisite baby food, that was Grandma's proudest dish. Grandma wasn't just about feeding the clubwomen. She understood the importance and joy of feeding the future. Of feeding our daughters. And she wanted me to know it, too.

For Grandma social justice began in the kitchen. And it extended to the garden. The equality she could achieve for her offspring was at her table and on her spoon. And in her yard.

She lived to be ninety-eight years old. By the end the closest she came to entertaining those who were not family was allowing children from the neighborhood to steal fruit from her plum tree. The day she died, she was tending the garden that allowed her to host, and uplift, without cooking.

Nana

JOAN MARIE BONTEMPS WILLIAMS

(1927-1998)

By 1968, the year Avon Williams was elected as the first black state senator in Tennessee since Reconstruction, everyone in historically black North Nashville knew their revolution had a chief cook and bottle washer, and her name was Joan.

They also knew that the civil rights movement in Nashville had a kitchen and that kitchen had an address, 1818 Morena Street, the home of Joan and Avon Williams.

What most didn't know was the revolution had a cookbook collection.

And so they didn't know that Joan, the person who funded and curated the cookbook collection, also financed hunks of the revolution—giving the civil rights movement in Nashville a particular flavor.

In other cities, civil rights leaders were feted with Sunday-preacher's-coming favorites: fried chicken and potato salad washed down with sweet tea. In Nashville, national and local civil rights leaders got their drink on and feasted on bar food.

When Alberta and Arna Bontemps's oldest daughter, Joan Marie, married Avon Williams, Jr., the strikingly handsome black attorney from Knoxville who was first cousin to Thurgood Marshall, at an elegant Nashville wedding (dissected and acclaimed in some circles for the next half-century) in 1957, most predicted Joan would soon retire from serving as university librarian and settle into being the kind of housewife-mother-hostess Grandma had been: persnickety, praiseworthy, praise-loving, and above all presiding high in an all-black bubble of formal elegance.

Joan and Avon had other plans.

They built a modern house smack-dab in the center of North Nashville, then flung open the doors to all and sundry. After they set up a bar with fancy glasses and top-shelf liquor, Joan got her food mill out and her blender plugged in.

Joan Williams loved to smash and pulverize. She turned livers into coarse chopped liver spreads and fine mousses. She mashed avocados into guacamole embellished with the unexpected—from canned pineapple to jarred salsa, when it first became available at the Kroger in Music City.

With her trusty blender, and eventually with one of the first home food processors in Nashville, she power-swirled fresh red and green bell peppers into jellies she would slather over mounds of cream cheese. She pureed canned tuna and canned salmon, then whipped it, with a simple balloon whisk and a strong arm, into a tasty tapenade to serve in a little crock and spread with a butter knife. Fresh basil from a friend's garden got whirled into Parmesan cheese and, presto-change-o, she had pesto, which she served with store-bought bread sticks.

Even yellow block cheese, smashed and lightened with red wine, sour cream, and her beloved mayonnaise, could take a star turn on the Morena

Street bar top—once she rolled it into a ball that was then rolled in crushed walnuts.

A busy woman who kept her doors open to all comers, Joan had a fine appreciation for the cheap and easy.

Joan loved anything you could smear across a cracker; loved any finger food that was hot with spice, hot with fire, and greasy; and she loved, loved, loved cold or room temperature, finger- or toothpick-friendly, crisp salty bits.

Nashville's iconic hot chicken is traditionally fried piece by piece, a slow and arduous process for a home cook trying to feed a crowd. Joan's hot chicken wings were simmered in butter and hot sauce. You could cook

Joan and Avon Williams flanked by supporters in Nashville, 1968. Avon had just won the Tennessee state senate race.

them cheap and quick by the vat. If she needed something cheaper and quicker, she'd serve dozens of perfectly boiled eggs tipped in salt.

In Nashville, at Joan's, seven days a week, twenty-four hours a day, it was always payday Friday night. Hard liquor flowed and tasty bites were served. And nobody got charged but Mr. and Mrs. Williams.

When I first met Joan in 1984 you could usually find her in her kitchen every hour from noon till midnight. There would be a pot of something, usually a bean chili, on the stove, a glass of scotch in her hand, and a new cookbook on a footstool at her knee.

Or maybe the cookbook would be in the hand that was not holding the scotch and she would be reading. In the back of the house, in the bedroom she shared with her husband, there would be two or three or more new cookbooks at the foot of her bed.

She seemed a woman of leisure. Her immersion in her cookbooks was an aspect of this performance.

When I first came to know the family, before I married the eldest child and only son, I, like most people who were not truly intimate with the inhabitants of 1818 Morena Street, thought Joan was a stay-at-home wife and mother. And I imagined she had always been large.

At just over five feet and carrying two hundred–plus pounds on her frame, she was substantial and handsome. Weight looked natural on her, like she had always been almost as wide as she was tall.

That couldn't have been further from the truth. A petite Negro beauty, Joan graduated first in her class at Fisk in 1949. She then went on to graduate studies, first in French at McGill University and then in library science at the University of Southern California. Upon graduating with a degree in library science, the still petite beauty served as a university librarian for two years at Maryland State University. Then she came back to Nashville, where she would meet and marry Avon and work as a librarian, for sixteen years at Fisk University and for twenty-two years at Tennessee State University. It was in the Avon years she picked up weight.

Too much worry, too much work, and too much whiskey will blow you up.

Civil rights lawyers in the South in the '60s didn't make much money. Many weeks it was Joan who brought home the bacon and fried it up in a pan, while reading of other pork in other places.

The same paycheck that allowed Joan to purchase expensive cookbooks made it possible for her to support her husband's efforts to bail out of jail the foot soldiers of the movement and to sue the state of Tennessee for providing inferior education to black children.

Joan worked hard to keep her labor as a librarian invisible. This was one of her rare concessions to black bourgeois respectability.

What else fell under most folks' radar? That cookbook collection.

The daughter of a famed librarian, Arna Bontemps, and a dedicated and long-serving university librarian herself, Joan Bontemps Williams became a collector of cookbooks.

At the time of her death, Joan's collection consisted of well over a thousand volumes. Slipped into her cookbooks were library card catalog cards, clean paper napkins, old bills, pages from mail-order catalogs, envelopes from her husband's law office, invitations, programs from luncheons, birthday cards, medical education sheets, and other ephemera she had placed to mark the presence of a recipe that intrigued her.

Baby's breath pressed between the pages of *The New World Encyclopedia of Cooking* was a delicate marker. On some of her sturdier bits and pieces she had written grocery lists, to-do lists, and menus. She was too much of a librarian to write in the actual books.

Most of her notes were on old library card catalog cards. Without marring a page with ink or food spatters, Joan left abundant traces of a loud and public life centered around feeding and entertaining family, friends, and a community of black politicos and civil rights combatants—while privately and quietly reading about food and collecting cookbooks—even as white supremacists bombed the home of her husband's law partner, Z. Alexander Looby, in 1960 and harassed her husband with death threats well into the '70s.

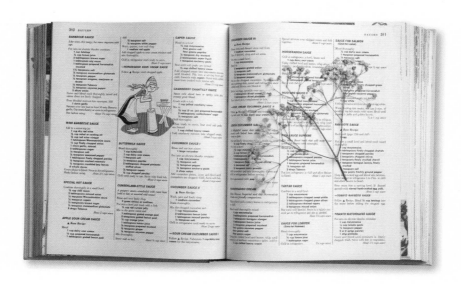

The New Encyclopedia of Cooking, from Joan's extensive cookbook collection.

She left the cookbook collection, in her will, to Caroline, her firstborn grandchild and only granddaughter.

When Caroline inherited the books, we had to buy bookcases to house them. We bought six cases, each with five shelves. We needed seven.

The oldest books in the collection are from the mid-1950s and inscribed "Joan Bontemps." The last books are from 1998, the year of her death.

Cooking from and with books freed Joan from the Southern roots of her kitchen. She created a new kitchen located squarely in Dixie (Nashville is the buckle of the Bible Belt) that exploded old parameters.

Title by title, recipe by recipe, dish by dish, cooking from *The Can-Opener Cook Book* and *The Peasant Kitchen: A Return to Simple, Good Food*, from *Annemarie's Personal Cook Book,* written by Annemarie Huste, former chef to the household of Jacqueline Kennedy, and *Palm Beach Entertains*, from *Chinese Regional Cooking* and any of the one thousand other cookbooks she owned, Joan defeated stereotypes used to confine the black woman's kitchen to something learned experientially, something handed down mother to daughter, cook to cook.

Her cookbook collection staked her claim to a specific and immense territory of culinary knowledge as her own. She both owned the volumes and possessed the knowledge within them. This twinned ownership became a central aspect of her identity. While remaining rooted to black Southern country cooking, hard-times-in-Harlem cuisine, and the fare of intellectual black expatriates abroad, she formed significant new culinary alliances.

By reading about food, Joan, who spent most of her waking hours in her kitchen, connected her kitchen to ones across the nation, across the world—particularly in England, France, and China—and across time.

She defined her kitchen not by the dishes she cooked but by the pages she owned, and pages she read.

The act of cookbook collecting allowed Joan to hide in plain sight her identity as a librarian. The presence of the books throughout the house, though perhaps invisible to most others, were highly visible to Joan. She knew where each volume was and what its placement meant. She understood that she was creating an archive of significance.

In the 1980s Joan and Avon renovated 1818 Morena Street, doubling the size of their house by creating a huge kitchen complete with fireplace, sitting areas, dining area, and bar. Over a third of the house was kitchen space.

Between the back door of the house and the fireplace in the kitchen/ great room they added a guest toilet, where Joan housed her Junior League cookbooks.

She conscripted the pretty spiral-bound volumes into the service of political statement. The Junior League volumes provided decoration, potty reading, and, shelved where they were, a healing belly laugh to anyone whose mama's mama had worked as a domestic or in a master's kitchen. Who but a brown girl who graduated summa cum laude from Fisk in 1949, and Arna Bontemps's firstborn child, would think to create retribution with a simple act of locating a category of books?

In no small part, Joan was the woman cookbooks grew. And I believe she understood her large body to be a reminder of liberating cooking adventures with her pages and her pots.

After Caroline was born, Joan told me she had consciously chosen to eat *whatever* and *as much as* she wanted. Independent of size. It was a point of personal freedom. Not cooking when she didn't have to was another point of personal freedom.

Though Joan and her mother, Alberta, were both great cooks, there is little overlap in their menus or kitchen habits. Alberta developed her kitchen skills through the discipline of providing a daily family meal at a set time. Joan developed strategies to avoid both the drudgery and the monotony she associated with formal family meals.

In Joan's house everyone ate at separate times. Very rarely did the family sit down to a meal together. This was considered a mark of freedom and a celebration of individuality and pragmatism. For years, at Joan's house, you ate when you were hungry.

If Grandma reveled in entertaining a large circle of women friends, Joan reveled in finding ways to split cooking chores with a close circle of women friends. Some of her best friends were large; most were not. Many were black women integrating white worlds and feeling the push of white aesthetics. Joan consciously resisted that pressure.

Her closest women friends—physicians, teachers, executives—and their families would typically eat at least one catch-as-catch-can meal a week at Joan's house. Joan and her family ate, by specific appointment, at the home of two of her dearest women friends on a weekly basis. Sunday lunch and Monday night were at Leatrice McKissack's. Saturday lunch and dinner were at Jane Maxwell's—both when the children were young and when the children were grown.

Late in her life, Joan's husband, the man the world called Big Avon, the man who proudly claimed he had helped desegregate every major school system in Tennessee except Memphis, except Shelby County, developed diabetes and ALS.

The family traveled to the Mayo Clinic to confirm the diagnosis and to gather any information about available cutting-edge treatments. I found the diet suggested for Big Avon by the Mayo Clinic tucked into the pages of the *Handbook of Holiday Cuisine.*

In an audacious and successful effort to extend her husband's life beyond what science predicted was possible, Joan began cooking Avon three plain and square meals a day, seven days a week.

The man who for years ate when he was hungry now was served precisely on the tick of a tock. And he was fed by a wife who, when push came to shove, allowed herself to be shackled to a kitchen clock.

And that wasn't all. Joan, the queen of exotic bar food, became the empress of bland food.

Avon moved his law practice into Joan's kitchen. Clients had always come to the door, and been fed, before and after office hours. Now they came any hour of the day all the days of the week, as did secretaries, and other lawyers, the phalanx of black folk that kept Senator Williams hard at work when his body betrayed him. And white people came, too, men who would be governor or mayor, state senators, country music folk, and even the great Southern food writer John Egerton.

Some things didn't change. Joan and the rest of the family still stuck mainly to bar food, only they started calling it *tapas*. Joan bought more cookbooks, read more cookbooks.

More things changed. The Supreme Court awarded Avon Williams a substantial fee for decades of unpaid civil rights work. Joan turned sixty-five in 1992 and retired from working outside her home as a librarian. The woman who had once ordered cookbooks (for example, *Thoughts for Buffets* and *Thoughts for Festive Foods*) from the Book-of-the-Month Club now ordered Raymond Oliver's *La Cuisine* from Kitchen Arts & Letters on Lexington Avenue, a bookstore frequented by New York's finest chefs, food historians, and food writers.

Eventually she added a daughter-in-law, me, to the list of folks she began to conscript to cook for the family. Before I knew it, she had me venturing various cioppinos and marinated chicken kebabs. For a while I was a part of making her cookbook dreams a reality. This was an act of love.

And this was an act of greater love: when life pressed in, meals at 1818 Morena Street became practical, pragmatic occasions, even as Joan's reading about meals became increasingly global, multicultural, esoteric, elegant, and adventurous.

Four generations (*from left*):
Alice Randall, Joan Bontemps
Williams, Caroline Randall Williams,
and Alberta Bontemps, 1988.

Mama

ALICE RANDALL

I've been searching for Diddy Wah Diddy for fifty-odd years.

Motown, circa 1964. There was no sink or refrigerator, but an Easy-Bake Oven and a jelly jar of water turned a windowless basement storage space into my very first kitchen.

Every dacquoise, Sacher torte, Siena cake, king cake, flaming baked Alaska, baba au rhum, Cointreau yeast cake, twelve-layer strawberry cake, crepe stack, and plain pound cake I have ever baked began in that room.

Brown powder transformed into something liquid like mud, which, after a trip through the lightbulb-powered stove, one layer at a time, transformed into a warm brown cloud I could eat.

I couldn't stop baking. With thin arms, I was, at age four, what my Daddy called "skinny as a mosquito in a wrastlin' jacket." I tore open multiple packets. I ate what I cooked. Then one day I didn't. Didn't eat what I cooked. Didn't follow the directions and bake two layers. I imagined a new cake. One day I baked four spongy chocolate disks.

As I mixed water with brown powder until I was stirring thick frosting, then assembled my layers on a purple plastic-filigree dessert plate, the sweet and acrid smell of cocoa powder filled the air. Soon the disks became a layer cake and my basement kitchen became a place of magical, radical metamorphosis.

But that wasn't the best part.

I baked in a basement room adjacent to my aunt's sewing room. This aunt—we called her "Sister"—owned the small apartment building where she, my parents and I, and a few other tenants lived.

Sometimes Sister would want to spend time out in the yard. More than once she offered me a small jar of maraschino cherries and invited me to climb up in her cherry tree. I accepted both.

More often Sister spent whole days and many weeks sewing me beautiful dresses with coats that matched. While she sewed, I baked.

One of my first vivid memories is the day I presented Sister, an early-retired seamstress whose prime pleasures were listening to Billie Holiday and sewing for me, with that saucer-size four-layer frosted cake I'd whipped up in my kitchen. She was dressed in a pastel negligee topped by a sheer matching robe. Her feet were bare. A cigarette hung from her mouth. I was dressed in the perfectly clean, perfectly pressed shirt and shorts outfit—perfectly matched to my shoes, my socks, and my hair bows—she had put me in that morning.

Sister had lost her only child in a tragic accident, a house fire. And she had lost the man she loved to cancer. I didn't know that then. I knew she didn't like to be interrupted in her sewing room. I knew she did so many sweet things for me yet seldom smiled.

I took my little chocolate cake in to Sister, she looked up from the

Randall siblings nightclubbing with their
significant others. *From left:* Helen Randall Gresham,
Jimmy Randall, Jimmy's date, Mary Frances
"Sister" Randall, George Randall, George's date,
and Ted Gresham. Detroit, circa 1955.

sewing machine, and she smiled. She ate the cake and she smiled. I went
back into my kitchen. I had made Sister smile.

I have not forgotten the dark aroma of dried oregano that rose from
the plastic bowl when you stirred water into the red-black powder and
made sauce for pizza. I remember, too, the thrill of putting soft pale
dough into the oven, pulling out a crispy brown disk, saucing it up, and
serving my pizza to Sister. Again she smiled. Food had power.

I was a Detroit girl, born in 1959, the same year as the Ford Galaxie, an automobile named to celebrate the space race. My Alabama-born daddy would drive me out in the middle of the night to see the shifts change. When car plants, like River Rouge, ran 24/7 employing 100,000 men, many of them black, all of them by Dixie sharecropping standards rich and safe, it was a sweet sight for a brown girl to see thousands going in and thousands going out with dark chins held high.

My daddy knew which number his car was off the assembly line. And so I figured this out easy: my kitchen was my smile factory.

I have had many kitchens since that first one in Detroit, Michigan. I built myself kitchens in Washington, D.C.; Cambridge, Massachusetts; Washington, D.C., again; Nashville, Tennessee; Alexandria, Virginia; Manila, the Philippines; Nashville again; New York, New York; Fort-de-France, Martinique; and Nashville again—all of them makeshift, all of them smile factories.

My current kitchen, in Nashville, is a hodgepodge miracle.

Before we bought it, the people who had renovated our hundred-year-old brick foursquare ran out of money prior to finishing the culinary spaces. They slapped in the bare minimum of appliances and slapped up just enough white laminate cabinetry to sell the place.

When we purchased it in 2000, the plan was to haul in a refrigerator and go without a garbage disposal until we "did" the kitchen.

There's still no garbage disposal and those cabinets are pulling away from the wall, but every time I step on the-cream colored tiles that will never get completely clean, I believe I have arrived in the vicinity of my version of Diddy Wah Diddy.

Diddy Wah Diddy is a mythical locale in African American folklore where there's abundant food and the food is always good. Gossip had it that in Diddy Wah Diddy the chickens ran around already cooked with a fork and knife in their back. Bo Diddley sang about Diddy Wah Diddy, calling it out by name in a 1956 single released by Checker Records. Decades before, Zora Neale Hurston wrote about this magic place where delight, and deliverance, is on every tongue and surreal food beauty in every eye. Diddy Wah Diddy is a place where good food—and plenty of it—is an eclipsing compensation for a bad life.

It's been quite a few pounds, eventually too many pounds, and a lot of kitchens getting to Diddy Wah Diddy.

• • •

I lived through the Detroit riots in the summer of 1967 and the implosion of my parents' marriage that winter, culminating in a child-snatch that relocated me to Washington, D.C., in time to live through the D.C. riots in 1968.

I landed in Washington looking for a kitchen where I could cook myself back to the home I lost in Detroit, or at least to Diddy Wah Diddy, that magic food land my daddy talked and sang about.

I never found or created a kitchen that could get me back to Detroit and the smile factory, but I found three mentors who got me a few steps on down the road: Julia Child, Craig Claiborne, and Irma Rombauer.

I had first encountered Child on television. We called it educational television back then, not public TV, and most everything was in black and white. It would have been about 1965.

As an only child I was often left home alone on pale wall-to-wall carpet in front of a floor-model Zenith television set in a "Mediterranean" carved wood cabinet. With little sense of humor and some curiosity, I became addicted to Michigan educational television and spent hours glued to the set, learning to lip-read (there was a course on that). And somehow I stumbled on a few episodes of *The French Chef.* From the first I loved Child's voice. I loved her intensity and her calm. I was fascinated by all the foods on the screen that I had never seen in real life or tasted.

Weaned on Dear's black Baptist Vacation Bible School theology and my black Lutheran parochial school's *Memory Book,* I knew there were worlds beyond the world I was living in—heaven and hell—but I wasn't intrigued. I prayed too much to go to hell. And I had already tasted milk and honey. What else was there?

Fancy food world. Julia Child's food captivated me. Big time. My infant culinary dreams were colonialized.

I wanted to taste mousse. Bullwinkle crossed with a chocolate bar is what I imagined. Little girl me thought an edible moose was hilarious. Food gave me my sense of humor.

Relocated to Washington, D.C., I quickly encountered the dishes of my Detroit dreams and television screens. It was the only thing that had improved in my life, so I ran with it. In my new life with flameless electric ranges and flickering countertop blenders, Paw Paw's fears seemed archaic.

My mother landed a political job and a prominent boyfriend. We moved into a big ramshackle house that had once been a diplomatic residence. She loved life in Washington. I loved cooking and school.

Soon I was studying the Vikings in social studies and cooking a barley stew like what I imagined the Vikings ate and getting my new friends to slurp it down with me.

Claiborne's *New York Times Menu Cookbook* was one of the few cookbooks on the shelves of the Takoma Park branch of the D.C. public library, where I did much of my homework from fifth through ninth grade. I checked it out. Never did return it. My mother paid the fee and I cooked from those pages weekly until I went to college. A mid-century blue-covered copy of *Joy of Cooking* bumped my hand when I was digging in the back of a deep kitchen drawer once owned by the government of Czechoslovakia. It became my middle-school cooking bible.

Before I knew it, I was cooking blackberry crepes for my weekend breakfasts and lusting after other fancy white European food.

By the time I graduated from Georgetown Day School, lemon soufflé, suprême de volaille Véronique, and dacquoise were staples in my home-cooking repertoire. I had forgotten, not to remember for a very long time, hog head cheese, plugs of juicy watermelon, fried bologna with hot sauce, and Coney Islands. Forgot all that.

It was a dream come real when I did an independent study with Julia Child at Harvard in the 1970s. Walking into her kitchen, sitting in her front room, talking with her and dissecting how and why the meal of high tea disappeared from America in the nineteenth century, was almost as magical as dress-box apples.

Every culinary extravaganza or carefully sourced culinary simplicity I have ever cooked up in one of my many kitchens—every coulibiac, every ceviche, every artichoke forest, every blini, every beef Wellington, every gravlax, every wild- and line-caught salmon, every heritage ham, every roasted perfect chocolate pepper—was a step or misstep on my road to Diddy Wah Diddy, where food dreams came true and we ate our way to happily ever after, forkful after forkful, pound upon luscious brown pound.

• • •

I can trace the evolution of my waistline in single dish: trifle.

The first trifle I ever tasted was made with Sara Lee pound cake, strawberry jelly, Jell-O brand instant vanilla pudding, canned fruit cocktail, and Reddi-wip. It was a Motown dish an elementary school child could assemble without adult supervision or danger. As I moved into middle school in D.C., I was trusted at the stove. Through trial and error and with assistance from the *The Joy of Cooking,* I learned to bake pound cakes, make cornstarch puddings, abandon Reddi-wip for Cool Whip, then learned how to whirl heavy cream into real whipped cream with the help of an electric mixer. Baking cakes and custards from scratch, I became particular about what I put in my mouth. I began to want my fruits to taste like something and not just be sweet and slippery. I started making my own fresh fruit salad with what was available, often strawberries and banana. By the time I graduated from college, my Christmas trifle featured luscious summer fruit flown in from South America and marinated in liqueurs. Around this same time I began to decorate the top of the trifle with sugared violets and roses imported from Europe and home-blanched, then carefully toasted, almonds.

A trifle like that was the dessert I made for Caroline's christening lunch in New York City in the winter of 1987, after her baptism at Grace Episcopal Church in Greenwich Village. It was the beginning of an end.

I had delivered Caroline at about 186 pounds in Nashville. When she was three weeks old, her father and I moved to New York. Walking the streets of Chelsea with Caroline in a Snugli, large didn't feel powerful. Large felt irrelevant.

It felt like a betrayal of Dear and Grandma and Joan to think that. So I started losing weight without thinking about large feeling irrelevant. I just bought myself a copy of Edward J. Safdie's *Spa Food,* prayed for Joan's good wishes, started cooking diet muffins and fish sausages, enrolled in an aerobics class, and promised myself I would walk in my neighborhood or dance around my living room for thirty minutes every day. A year and a few months later, I was smaller—the smallest I would be in adult life. But I kept cooking from my standard repertory for my husband and our friends, so trifle was still on the menu. My weight would zigzag up and down, each upswing hitting a new high for the next twenty-five years.

Caroline was three when Avon and I divorced in 1991. Grandma showed her feminist stripes when I told her the marriage was ending, standing by her stove and saying, "We women have to stand together." I couldn't have loved the lady or her largeness more.

As a young single mother with a career and a baby, I stopped baking pound cake and had no time to source and prep elaborate fruit salads. I substituted a locally made cake and started poaching pears in red wine for a simple but still fancy fruit that was naturally sweet. The sugared flowers disappeared but the almonds remained (only I stopped blanching and toasting them myself). I still made the custard and the mounds of whipped cream until I realized, one, I didn't have the time; two, I was too fat; three, I didn't want my daughter eating any of it—the whipped cream or the custard or all that cake. I wanted Caroline to inherit a very different kitchen from the one I inherited. I wanted health as well as history on the table.

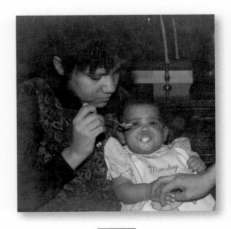

Caroline takes her first bite of solid food with her mother, Alice. Washington, D.C., 1988.

Caroline was almost ten when I married David Ewing in 1997. We had Grandma's blessing. In fact, Avon's family match-made me to David. And Avon and David were friends until Avon's death in 2005.

Not long after my wedding to David, my mother was diagnosed with cancer. Taking the walk with my mother to her grave, I ballooned to well over two hundred pounds.

Part of it was exhaustion. Helping her was every kind of extra work. Black women are not fat because we are lazy; we are fat because we are tired. Sleep deprivation is a large part of the fat-food puzzle that is too often overlooked. Not getting enough sleep was part of blowing me up. And part of it was that my husband thought I was beautiful large. And I thought I was beautiful large—because I looked more like Dear. But more than that, I found it necessary to be large if I was going to face my childhood. My mother had been a criminally abusive mother. I coped with the trauma of assisting her by applying the mood stabilizer Dear had prescribed: sugar.

I didn't suck a sugar tit or swill sweet tea—but I ate a lot of pasta, too many bagels, every kind of cracker, midnight bowls of ice cream, and my fair share of vodka tonics. The carbs calmed me. I buried my mother with care, every possible consideration, and very, very fat.

And I buried her on the farm that had been in David's family since the end of slavery.

In 2001 I found myself with borderline high blood pressure, scared of dying, and in therapy looking for a foodway forward that wouldn't sacrifice the legacy of my foremothers. I realized that "a deuce and a quarter" was supposed to be the nickname for a car, the Buick Electra 225, not the weight of a woman. Particularly not a five-foot-two woman.

Something had to give.

Eventually all that was left of the trifle was the poached pear. It is a magnificent remnant.

In my lifetime I have poached over a thousand pears. When I am choosing the wine, the foundation of my poaching liquid, I look for something inky purple, something structured enough to hold dark and bright notes even after being boiled with cinnamon and clove and lemon, which can flatten and make insipid many worthy grapes. I am thinking about creating a jewel. I am thinking, once I peel the pear, there is a roughness to the flesh that will grip this red and this blue and leave the surface shining and penetrated. If I poach it right, you will see into the thing, or at least believe you can. When your spoon pierces the flesh of your pear and you scoop yourself a taste, through to the seed and to the core, all will be inky purple. Intoxicated with the beauty of this purple, you will see the bottom-heavy shape that celebrates women with proud large asses.

There are a thousand reasons why I love poached pears. But the three that are most important are these: they remind me of Dear's dress-box apples; they remind me of Sister's maraschino cherries; and the most important, peeling pears together has given me hundreds of hours to talk with my daughter.

My kitchen is where I have told my daughter all my most important secrets and stories.

Told her about kitchen rapes I have told you about, and that I have not told you about. In my kitchen I confessed to my daughter that I weighed over two hundred and twenty-five pounds. She wasn't surprised about how much I weighed, but she was surprised that I planned to try to do something about it. And it was in my kitchen that I made her promise me that she would help me get on the treadmill every day. Loud and proud, I promised her that I would do all in my power to be the last fat black woman in our family by helping her reinvent, reimagine, and remix the foodways legacies she had inherited.

And it was in my kitchen that I told her the rest of the story about Sister.

An Easy-Bake Oven and maraschino cherries were not the only food-related gifts Sister gave me.

The first truly delicious thing I ever ate was a warm apricot from a tree in her Detroit backyard. I still remember the sweet and heat of the flesh, the fur of the skin against my lips, the slight vibration when my teeth hit the hidden hard stone. That apricot was a full-on, taste and tactile, mouth pleasure.

Quiet as it's kept, the truth is that black folk were growing food in Detroit long before the world learned to call the city Motown. In 1963, on a street called Parkside, and on a lot of other streets, there were little orchards.

Sister had five fruit trees where we lived, right next to the freeway in downtown Detroit. I truly believe somehow being near the freeway, a symbol for her of modernity, of progress, of safety, made it possible for her to grow those trees. And the fact that apricots didn't grow in Alabama probably helped, too.

Sister said a garden was God's own kitchen. Said she didn't need a stove to feed me. She was Dear's daughter, so she didn't go much in a regular kitchen. I didn't pay attention. I wanted a stove to feed my Barbie dolls. An Easy-Bake Oven. I told her so.

If that exquisite apricot had been the only or even the primary food gift Sister had given me to eat that summer, I might have been a thinner woman today. But it was not all she gave me. She gave me the Easy-Bake Oven and the maraschino cherries.

But more than those gifts there was that apricot, a good taste on a healthy tongue. And in telling me nature was God's own kitchen, Sister told me the kitchen was an important place. A sacred place. A place worthy of my efforts. She got all that right.

The power of a warm, raw food. A truth with roots in Africa. When I remembered Sister's best food gift, when I finally started really thinking about my great-grandmother Betty's farm, provoked in part by visits to David's family farm, and not just thinking about Dear's exile from it, I invited the garden into my kitchen and arrived at my very own Diddy Wah Diddy.

It's not a place where the chickens run around cooked with forks and knives in their backs. That is the dream of someone from a different time—of a people who have had the joy of cooking for themselves at their own fire stolen from them. A dream of food in abundance to excess is a dream of a young pregnant woman in the bowels of a ship crossing the Middle Passage who doesn't know when her next mouthful will be.

Diddy Wah Diddy now is all about pleasure and safety. Our kitchen engages all five senses. That is a Diddy Wah Diddy thing. And it is also a Diddy Wah Diddy thing that the senses provoke memory. And provoking memory is not always an easy thing in the black American world. My Diddy Wah Diddy kitchen is a place where it is safe to remember all—all endured, all desired, all lost, all treasured, all treasured and lost—precisely because the Diddy Wah Diddy kitchen bombards tongue, eye, ear, fingertips, and nose with pleasure.

Hatch Show Print
party invitations adorning the
kitchen of our home on Blair
Boulevard in Nashville.

What else makes up my Diddy Wah Diddy dream kitchen?

An ugly upright piano that loves to stay in tune. Caroline plunked her way from do-re-me to Mozart on its keys. A wall papered with poster-size Hatch Show Print invitations for parties we've given, with illustrations of blackberries, thyme, wild ginger, pears, and other ingredients from feasts past that bloom in oversize splendor in all seasons of the year, reminding us of guests we love, guests we've lost, and guests we must invite again soon.

Our dining room table seats eighteen and it is often full. Our library table sits six. The kitchen table, a white wood door set on sawhorses and covered in glass (the better to roll out pastry), seats ten—when it's not being called into use as a buffet table for the dining room and library. Several times a year we invite thirty-four for dinner. Two or three times most years we feed about two hundred, mostly sitting down. People take shifts. One year arriving guests were asked to reserve one of four time slots in one of four rooms. That was the year we sat people in our bedroom on the high tester bed. Only in a surreal magical food dream come true could a funky little kitchen with one tiny oven, four electric eyes, handle all that easily.

And speaking of easy, there's been help in my kitchen. Martha, Elena, Joyce, Rebekkah, and Daniela, white girls all, have worked for me and mine. Elena, Joyce, Rebekkah, and Daniela cranking out the day-to-day meals, one year or another. Martha assisting with the festival meals. All of these women doing something, even if it was just a little something, to honor and start paying down the cultural debt, the principle that can never be gotten down to, of all the years of black women working in white women's kitchens. There's reparation in my kitchen.

And crossroads. We've fed Tea Party activists and Promise Keepers as well as members of the ACLU and the NAACP and MoveOn.org. Strangers arrive, share—perhaps a common cocktail and a common pear— and often leave understanding, somehow, they are connected to each other.

If it is spring, pink roses, cut from a rosebush that threatens to pull off a side of our house, fill my kitchen with a scent of spice, melon, musk, and memories of Dear's rose garden. Any time of year you may catch scent from my tea drawer. I love teas that wear their drama way up front and loud—be it smoky Lapsang Souchong and Russian Caravan or the full-flower frenzy of Mariage Frères Un Soir de France.

There's some tangible treasure, too: Joan's cookbooks that Caroline inherited. They live in my house waiting to move into hers.

But first the collection became Caroline's cooking school, much as it had once been Joan's. The inaugural grand feast the two of us cooked using Joan's cookbook library was a Christmas breakfast for about a hundred in 2000. Caroline was thirteen years old.

Before we knew it we were peeling and poaching more than a hundred pears in red wine in a nonreactive metal pot and we were weighting down a layered vegetable terrine molded in a bread pan with a piggy bank, all the while turning Joan's pages and learning why and how and getting inspired to cook with the ghost of Joan and recipes from *Dinner at Buckingham Palace* and many other volumes.

As we eventually understood Joan's cookbook collection to be a syllabus, we saw from the first that it was an act of claim staking. As we have continued to cook with the books over a decade, we have discovered ourselves more and more involved with and engaged by our encounters with Joan's culinary curiosity and imagination.

What did she make of a golden turkey, roasted and then literally gilded? What does it mean that she gifted us with a picture of that? And if there is a card slipped in beside it, does that mean anything?

The Englishwoman's Kitchen (1983, edited by Tamasin Day-Lewis) was a book at Joan's knee that perplexed me when I first met her. I wondered what a cookbook full of recipes from noblewomen had to do with Joan. Rereading it recently, I came upon a "Feast Fit for Judges" and knew that would be a meal Joan would have enjoyed cooking for her husband before he fell ill—even though, or perhaps precisely because, he was not in the end appointed federal judge because he refused to play low, refused to allow one of the ones who was appointing him to call him by his first name.

Other questions raised by cooking with Joan's books: Was our love of and recognition of crowns—regal dishes that show loved ones how much we esteem them, just like Alberta had once done—seeded by our reading from Joan's library? Maybe. What I know for sure: her collection contained cookbooks that drew me back to my food roots before Child, Claiborne, and Rombauer.

In the pages of Freda DeKnight's *A Date with a Dish,* we discovered the Little Brown Chef. For me and for many this is the black *Joy of Cooking.* Also from Joan's shelves: *Spoonbread and Strawberry Wine,* written by the Darden sisters, who tell through recipes and remembrances the history of an accomplished black Alabama family; *A Good Heart and a Light Hand*—subtitled *Ruth L. Gaskin's Collection of Traditional Negro Recipes,* with a striking black-and-white portrait of Mrs. Gaskin, large, dark, and lovely, standing at a stove, pot on burner, spoon in hand, on its cover—opened a window into a soft side of politics-by-recipe while providing recipes that took us back to the twentieth-century basics. *Gene Hovis's Uptown Down Home Cookbook*—with Hovis, dapper in a bow tie and blue pinstriped suit on the cover, along with a blurb from Claiborne—was a book on Joan's shelves that reminded me to look high and low for black foodways.

Joan was a renegade. She refused to embrace only black foodways or Eurocentric white foodways. With her cookbook collection she said without words: All this is yours. Choose what you want from it. It was Joan who taught us that all that is freedom food is soul food. And all that enslaves us is poison.

Now I say it loud and proud. *All that enslaves us is poison.* I say it inflected with Dear's fear of the kitchen and Grandma's love of entertaining. I say it influenced by Sister's little orchard. I say it still knowing that deliciousness can keep you from going crazy—but it has got to be a healthy delicious or you'll be sane and dead.

It took a hundred years of cooking in this family to arrive here—to get to Caroline's love of the sufficient and sensual, to put aside compensatory excess—but we've arrived at a green black place, Caroline's kitchen.

Baby Girl

CAROLINE RANDALL WILLIAMS

I'm a Southern girl. Georgia and Alabama are my blood. Nashville is my home. Mississippi is my right now. And us Southern girls, we're supposed to be able to *cook*. And by cook, I don't mean follow a tidy little recipe or warm something up; I mean feed your family and friends in mind and body and everything else with things that are delicious and not give two blinks about how healthy they are. Except that when you love your family, you want them to live—and live well. In some ways, my story is the story of so many black women, so many proud home cooks and homemakers. I don't have enough fingers and toes to count the number of people in my family who have gotten fat and sick from what modern memory remembers as "soul food."

But all that is only the smallest part of the tale I'm telling. What I want to share with you, really, is my kitchen now, because my kitchen now is the happiest restoration project in the world. I'm sanding and polishing and shining and refinishing the house that past home cooks built. I'm keeping the foundations, throwing out the junk, and renovating the rest. A family home restored to new and greater glory.

My mother and I spent the summer of 2013 in our kitchen reinventing our family's foodways. Mama did it for me and for her. I did it for Mississippi.

In 2010, I moved to the Delta to teach school for two years. The way I cooked, the way I ate, was only one of a number of adjustments I confronted. But it was a big one. I was raised in restaurants, and when it *was* time to cook, I was raised to go to well-stocked specialty grocery stores, farmer's markets, even the farms themselves. In the Delta, almost without exception, the best groceries—the only groceries—come from Walmart. They have the widest selection, with the freshest vegetables—these days they're often locally sourced—and the consistency isn't matched anywhere else in the region. Let me just take this moment to say, after three years of living in Mississippi, that I love Walmart. It has changed my life. With its produce aisle as my only grocery store, I learned how to eat healthfully *and* soulfully, day in and day out, on a teacher's budget.

My students ate lots of takeout: Popeye's chicken, ribs from Boss Hog's, pizza from Subway (yes, they make pizza). And their choices, restaurant-wise, were my only choices, too. If I wanted to keep the healthy body I'd fought for my whole life, I needed another option. One Sunday evening I finally swallowed my prejudice, and me and my high horse took our behinds to Walmart. I needed quick-cooking high-quality food, and I didn't want it to be frozen. So I bought myself a big ol' stockpot, some bags of broccoli, and some chicken breasts. When I got home, I threw it all in a colander, and guess what? I had lunch and dinner for a week. Good lunch and dinner.

"What you got to eat today, Miss Williams?" That's what my students started to ask me, the day I decided to experiment with garlic powder and cayenne. "You fix that chicken? Bring me some." It smelled like home cooking. It got me through my days teaching and not only did I *not* compromise on the healthiness and quality of my food, but I also found for both myself and my students a simple truth: food that talks to your soul can be made with the inexpensive ingredients and tools that some of our grandmothers used to look after their families—and still be clean and fast.

I remember a student asking me one day, "Miss Williams, why you always try to eat so healthy?" The question startled me. And impressed. It got to the heart of the matter.

I had watched my mother struggle with her weight. Growing up, most of my family was large. My mother thought I was perfect just the way I was and let me eat whatever I wanted; she, at the time, was still fairly petite. When I was around ten or eleven, the tables started turning. I started playing soccer, and wanting to eat food that would be good fuel, while my mother piled on the weight. I saw her become heavier and heavier without any real concern—she was just following the model of the many women in our family who came before her. I continued to keep a careful watch on my own eating, and my own size, throughout school, knowing I didn't even have the luxury my mother had had, of being skinny as a child. I was average, "healthy"—never tiny.

It wasn't until my mom reached her largest, and I witnessed how hard it was for her to try to do something about it, that I really began to worry. I wondered why I hadn't said something to her sooner. I started to contemplate what it would be like if she didn't change, and to ask myself what kind of grandmother she would or even could be, if something didn't change. And as for my own body, I realized that a real commitment to my lifelong vigilance had to begin *now* if I wanted to stay healthy for the rest of my life. If I let my guard down, it would be hard to come back from that. So hard I didn't even know if my extraordinary mother could do it and keep it done.

I didn't tell my student all of that. "I'm trying to take care of my body," I told her.

"I hear that," she said. "Feel like I can't never get rid of this belly but seem like I can't figure out what to eat." We talked about how her family discouraged her from dieting. More girls joined in the conversation.

I invited her to try my chicken. She looked at it suspiciously, but took a bite. "Is it good?" some of the other girls asked, skeptically. "Yeah!" she said. "It taste like *something*. I thought it wasn't gonna taste like *nothing*."

These days, that is always my goal: food that tastes like something and costs my health nothing.

My dear friend Ruthie Collins is the reason I survived my first year in a Delta classroom. Ruthie was the parent-teacher liaison at the school where I taught. There was a decade between us, but we were soul-mated sisters from the beginning. She cheered me through my first year of teaching and I helped her through her last year of college. We kept up even though I headed north to Oxford, Mississippi. Our two biggest ongoing conversations: how to get kids in the Delta educated, particularly the boys; and how to keep kids in the Delta from getting too big, particularly the girls.

And we talked a lot about our own eating and the way our families ate. One day she shared a conversation she had with her mother-in-law that changed how I looked at my family's foodways. Ruthie said she used to bake a pound cake once a week, but that her mother-in-law criticized her for it. Her mother-in-law said that when she was young, they had a pound cake at holidays, yes, but not every week! That was too much! It made the cake less special. That's when I had my little revelation: we've begun to mistake celebration food for everyday food.

When I think about what the future of food looks like, I find myself thinking that it looks like the past of Ruthie's mother-in-law more than it looks like the past of my grandmothers. Ruthie's mother-in-law knew that excess every day would spoil the real pleasures of a meaningful feast. And now I know it, too. After years of singing "Mississippi Goddam," I say: Mississippi saved my life.

• • •

I called my father's mother Nana—Joan, as you've met her in my mother's words. Her mother, Alberta, I called Grandma. My dad would take me to visit one or the other, or both of them, every Sunday. I would get there, and the first thing Nana would do would be to fix my wild hair, brushing it into puffs with her big old paddle brush, slicking it down with Vaseline, braiding it down my back. Then, nursing her scotch on the rocks all the while, she would feed me.

When Nana died, my cousin Aara recited a menu out loud, like a litany. She said, "I know how to make cheesecake, I know how to make shrimp, I can fix cornpone, potatoes." Nana didn't teach me how to cook—I was too little when she passed to be much use at a stove or with a chopping knife. What Nana taught me was how to take care of folks, and to eat.

Nana taught me that a guest should always feel welcome, and that it didn't take much to be ready for them except a sense of fun, a well-stocked bar, and enough food. It didn't have to be fancy, just tasty and plentiful. Nana's own mother, the elegant, firm Alberta—well, she might have married a Bontemps, but she didn't live *bontemps,* not like Nana did. Nana was *born* for good times. Nana, with her endless supply of snacks: The nuts! The bourbon balls! The stove top covered with pots steaming with any number of delicious things, just waiting to be heaped into bowls! And of course plenty of booze and card decks, so that anybody who felt like cutting loose was right at home in her kitchen, no matter the time of day or night. Even I had my own special cocktail: caffeine-free Coke with a splash (or three) of grenadine.

I knew I had entertaining in my blood from the first time I sat down with a plate of meatloaf and let my cousins teach me Spades in a room full of company. My sense of the old, right way, though? Well, that comes straight from Grandma Alberta and her layered cakes, her crystal, and her white tablecloths. Every surface had a perfectly ironed doily. The cookie jar was always full. The candy dish always held butterscotch, or those little red candies wrapped to look like strawberries. Even in her very old age, when Grandma couldn't cook much anymore, she would make sure that the chicken and biscuits we picked up from around the corner on Sunday afternoons were served on china plates and in silver baskets lined with cloths.

My mother's kitchen was and is a magical place. Cooking, for her, is a special event. There has always been a grand sense of ceremony about the times she chooses to grace the kitchen, something that I have found to be both a point of admiration and a source of frustration. My mom doesn't often lift a whisk or preheat an oven unless it is the beginning of a masterpiece meal. Otherwise, her kitchen remains pristine, her refrigerator uncluttered, her refined palate appeased in one of the many favorite restaurants we have in and around Nashville.

In my mom's kitchen I learned all the complicated, delicious, *we really shouldn't eat this every day but really want to eat this every day and will eat it way too often and way too much of it* food that I still treasure. I remember helping cook Thanksgiving, sitting for hours at the kitchen table peeling tiny pearl onions that my mother would simmer with just *heaps* of heavy cream, salt, and pepper. If the food wasn't for a holiday, it was often themed. One of my dearest memories is of a phase in which she announced that we were no longer eating dinner but having high tea. She showed me how to roll the plain white sandwich bread very thin, and cut off the crusts, to let the butter get to room temperature so we could spread it, to love the crunch and clean flavor of plain cucumbers and asparagus folded between the bread and butter. And then, of course, came the soup! In beautiful bowls patterned with pink flowers (bowls I use now in Mississippi) she would pour me soups of her own creation—some she'd learned and experimented with when she did her independent study of the English "tea" with Julia Child during her time at Harvard—and garnish them with edible flowers. Those meals are a childhood treasure to me.

During the week, growing up, we often had cooks, and they were always white women. There was Joyce, the vegan cook; Elena, the vegetarian hippie who made incredible pasta; Rebekkah, who was sweet and soulful; and Daniela, who was creative and sophisticated. But my mom was still the best. She made me the celebration food. One Christmas, I got a waffle maker that made heart-shaped waffles. I have memories of weekend nights watching my mom making waffle batter from scratch, and waking up the next morning to my mom buttering the waffle iron, and then letting me help pour the batter that had risen overnight. There was yeast in her favorite waffle recipe. It was nothing like out of a box. She made delicious French toast. In honor, I suspect, of Dear and her dress-box apples, Mama would go to our favorite grocery store, the Corner Market, and buy what I liked to call "fancy" pasta, handmade into whimsical shapes, and then she would dye it exciting colors before serving it to me, with chicken, or with pesto she would make herself, or with tomato sauce. Mama made me seven-layer strawberry cakes with cream cheese icing, and she made me the best brownies that anyone, anywhere, has ever eaten.

When Nana died of breast cancer in 1998, she left me her 1,500-book-strong collection of cookbooks, a love of food and of hosting, and a very real worry about how to eat for the "good times" and live for a long time. But starting in Mama's quirky kitchen and then on to a high school dorm and then a college one, my day-to-day kitchen practices were limited, despite my privileged exposure to good food.

And then, for my junior year of college I decided to study abroad. In January 2009 this Southern girl moved into a flat in Oxford, England. For the first time in my life, I was responsible for all of my own meals. It was slow going at first. In the adjustment to student life in my first apartment, I found I had no time for the celebration feasts of Nana's and Grandma's kitchens. And I certainly wasn't interested in trying to re-create the themed, carefully orchestrated, sporadic meals of my mother's kitchen. I ate a lot of sandwiches that first month. And a lot of pub food. And then, about two months into my eight-month stay, I moved into a larger flat, with roommates who turned out to be lifelong friends, and I started to cook. I bought lamb, looked up about a thousand recipes on the internet, and tried my hand at red wine sauce. Inspired by a beau, I made a successful attempt at poached salmon with leeks. My English friends were intrigued by Mexican food, so I made them guacamole.

Somehow, suddenly, the kitchen was no longer the elaborate to-do of my youth but a community effort in which I could cheerfully take part, somehow managing to please both my audience and myself. I learned how to attack the grocery store—a skill I've discovered few friends my age have had time or means to develop—so that I spent the least money and time but bagged the most nutrient-dense calories. Keeping in mind what I had at home, I went to vegetables first, thinking about how I could add them to my other ingredients. Spices became the treasure they were a thousand years ago, when people traded them for money. I flavored sweet potatoes with olive oil and rosemary one day and butter and nutmeg the next. Soon I found myself gathering friends together regularly, cooking great big dinners that we ate in the dining room, in the back garden, on picnics, or even in the kitchen. We shared recipes, and invented them. We figured out how to be young people enjoying one another's company in an environment we'd created, instead of having to rely on ready-made products.

After my semester in England, the dining hall back at college was a new world for me. I didn't have the kitchen I'd grown so attached to, but I had new, keen ideas for the healthy potential of the ingredients available. Plain tuna was all of a sudden appealing—wasn't that olive oil I saw at the end of the salad bar, and lemon juice next to it? Salt, pepper, a little dried tarragon? I began to innovate with the materials available, to see what familiar and nourishing flavors I could come up with, given the dining hall's limited resources. This little tuna salad recipe, for example, stuck with me, as you'll see in just a little bit. Nana loved tuna salad. It's sweet to remember her healthy impulses, precious and rare as they were.

• • •

That is what's hard, isn't it? To keep the good old—to remind others of what that is—and add new that fits.

The answer, for me, was to dig deep and figure out what we already had in our heritage toolbox that was enough. What are the simple ingredients that we ate when we had to labor with our hands all day, when we were too tired to fry things or wait for them to rise, when we were too poor to cover all our food in sugar and extra flour? What did we eat that we forgot we ate? Chicken. Spices. Herbs. Always got a use for sweet potatoes. Onions in the cupboard. Eggs. Olive oil and cayenne within reach from the stove. There's never a reason not to have those things around. A real quick meal is never far away.

It's time to remember a crucial truth: The foods we now think of as "soul food" are not the ones our families were eating day in and day out; they are the celebration foods that have claimed our attention over time. All that extra sugar, the flour, the cream—these things were luxuries. What were we eating, we have to ask ourselves, when we were working from can't see in the morning to can't see at night? Sustainable foods that sustained us. The food at the soul of our community, the food that kept us on our feet and marching forward, was clean and delicious, in many ways before its time. When I throw watermelon and tomatoes and avocado into a bowl and call it fruit salad, I'm calling back past the fruit cocktail, the sugar-covered cherries and pineapples, to that tradition of plain old goodness that is our real inheritance.

We can't all be urban farmers; we can't all shop only organic, or even at decent grocery stores. But we still have to ask ourselves what we are going to do about the way we eat, day to day. Yes, sometimes we live in food deserts. Sometimes the only grocery store is a Walmart. And that's okay. I've been there. Funnily enough, it was right in the middle of my Delta food desert that I learned that I could scratch my soul food itch and eat healthfully, too. When you walk through the main entrance of the Walmart in Greenwood, Mississippi, the first thing you see is the produce, and I finally started to pay attention to it. I grabbed the sweet potatoes. I grabbed the eggplants and tomatoes, and I figured out how to do the kind of mix-and-match shopping that made my cupboard and my refrigerator always make sense to me, always able to offer something up to sustain my body and soul when I was hungry.

These days, still a little to my surprise, I'm back in Oxford—the Mississippi one, this time. My new Oxford has been a whole other adventure altogether. If you come on to my house on a Sunday, I'm cooking, usually for a great big group—that's Nana at work in me. The china plates my friends are eating on? Those are all Grandma. The counter scrubbed within an inch of its life? I'll always do that for my mother. The healthy soul with the old-school spirit, though, is all me.

I'll never forget the first time I had a bunch of my friends over for roast chicken. I was working on the side dishes in the kitchen and had set the two chickens on the table. When I came back a few minutes later, no one had touched the chicken. "Ya'll go ahead and start!" I said, cheerfully. A sheepish smile passed around the table as one of my friends admitted to me, "None of us knows how to carve a chicken." My generation spends so much time glorifying food and taking pictures of it, that when it comes to actually handling homemade food, people are at a loss. "Just get in there with a knife!" I cried. Needless to say, when I returned with the roasted sweet potatoes, there was hardly any chicken left.

The number one thing you can do to improve your health is to cook at home. My future children are going to eat differently than I did as a kid. I ate out; my kids will eat in. I thought cooking was for special occasions; my kids will know cooking is for every day. I thought "soul food" was a guilty pleasure; my kids will know "soul food" is a healthy truth.

I'll want my kids to get underfoot in the kitchen. They will be brave and adventurous and know the flavors they like, and enjoy the experiment of creating them. When I have a family, we will know that vegetables don't happen by magic, and they don't just happen in grocery stores, that they can also happen in pots on a deck, in a raised bed, or in a small plot out in the yard.

There was a time, not long enough ago, when black people didn't have much that they could call theirs, save for the people they loved and what little food they could try to make special to put in their mouths. So when I say I know food is important to us, I mean it is indispensable, emotional, historical, and above all, precious. A pot of greens—washed seven times before cooking, one for each day God created the world and for the day he rested—was a way a mother could show love when she couldn't buy things. I want to keep that spirit. I want to keep those flavors, but I want to do it in a way that my children know their mama is looking out for their bodies as well as their souls.

And looking out for her own body, too. But I'm not a mama yet.

For now, standing on the shoulders of these brilliant, big, black women, I go on ahead and feed my friends from my small kitchen. I feed them from my history, from *our* history, our past, our present, and from the fresh start of what I hope our future looks like. And that, as we like to say in my family, is how you entertain like Mama and stay healthy like Baby Girl.

SIPS
&
BITES

PAW PAW'S CLEAN AND SOBER

DEAR'S SWEET FORGIVENESS

GRANDMA'S BELLINI

MAMA'S TEQUILA ICE

CAROLINE'S HOTTY TODDY

NANA'S MARTINI

PEPPER JELLY COINS

SOUTHERN HUMMUS

BLACK-EYED PEA HUMMUS

RED SPREAD

HOMEMADE SALSA WITH CUCUMBER CHIPS

BABA GHANOUSH

ROASTED PEPPERS WITH
SARDINES AND BOILED EGGS

GUACAMOLE

GEORGE WASHINGTON CARVER'S
HOMEMADE PEANUT BUTTER

PAW PAW'S
CLEAN AND SOBER

MAKES 6 DRINKS

Paw Paw didn't drink. He looked and acted like the kind of dashing tough guy one might expect to, though. When he left the house during any season but hot summer, he always wore a topcoat and a fedora. All seasons of the year he wore sharp suits. Pressed shirts. Flashy but somehow elegant jewelry.

There is a story often told in our family of how Paw Paw struck a man down with a crowbar because that man cursed in front of Dear. Nobody said "damn" or "hell" in front of any black lady when Paw Paw was around.

The man was often outnumbered but seldom outgunned. Paw Paw packed a pistol. In Detroit's Black Bottom he was a force of nature, a strong current in a rough river. There are several stories about Paw Paw that Mama tells often, but none more often than this:

"The very first time I ever encountered something I would have called 'racism,' had I known the word, I went to Paw Paw for justice. I couldn't wait to hear what he was going to do to the person who hadn't given me what I earned just because of the color of my skin. When I finished talking, he squatted down in front of me, looked me straight in the eye, took both my hands, and said, 'Be three times as good and have what you want.'"

For Paw Paw a big part of being three times as good was staying sober and alert, ready to pounce, from can't see in the morning to can't see at night.

This drink is a sober cousin to a mint julep. And of course it has the ice cubes he and Dear considered so much a miracle because they didn't own a "coolerator" until the 1950s. I love keeping a pitcher of this in my own coolerator to special-up a Mississippi afternoon.

1 cucumber

1 bunch fresh mint

1 lime

1 quart club soda, cold

1 Peel and slice the cucumber. Strip the leaves off of the mint stems. Rinse, then thinly slice the lime. Combine the cucumber, mint leaves, and lime slices in a large pitcher, then pour in 1 quart of water. Let sit in the refrigerator for at least an hour and preferably overnight.

2 To serve, fill highball glasses with ice cubes. Pour the infused liquid over the ice cubes, filling each glass two-thirds of the way, and then top with the club soda.

DEAR'S
SWEET FORGIVENESS

MAKES 1 DRINK

In her early marriage days, when Dear wanted to make a cocktail, she would take whatever cordial she had on hand, perhaps dewberry, and dilute it with soda water. She liked her drinks sweet, weak, seldom, and delicious.

Dear and Paw Paw had a grand love. Because he could not read or write, every day she would read his mail to him. One day a letter came that read, "I know you love wife, but we had son, and I can't take care of him anymore." Paw Paw walked off, ashamed. Dear didn't say a word. Instead she sent for that boy and raised him in Detroit with her own.

I do not keep dewberry cordial in the house, but there's usually a bottle of St.-Germain, the haunting floral liqueur. People seem to love to give me the statuesque, faceted, blue-labeled bottle that looks like perfume and drinks like a garden. I definitely do not mind.

We think this drink is almost as sweet as Dear's forgiveness.

1 finger of elderflower liqueur, such as St.-Germain

3 Dear's Ice Cubes (recipe follows)

1 cup sparkling water

In a rocks or old-fashioned glass, pour the elderflower liqueur over the ice cubes, and top off with the sparkling water. Serve and sip!

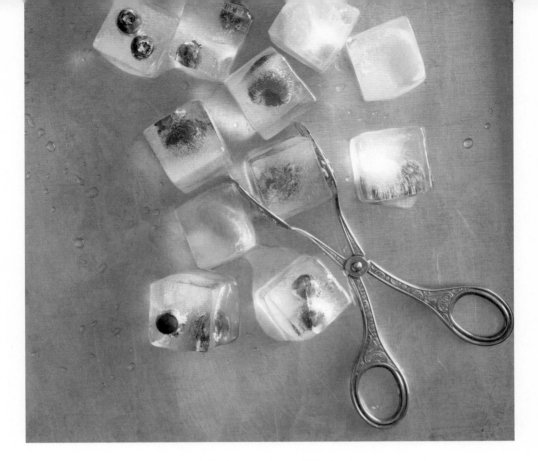

DEAR'S ICE CUBES

MAKES 12 ICE CUBES

Someone very precious to me once said out loud what Dear lived: "All you need to be healed of a heart hurt is love and time." These ice cubes require both. Only love will get you looking for perfect fruit to put into your ice trays, and it takes time once you put the ice trays into the freezer for the water to perform the simple everyday miracle of turning from liquid to solid.

Dear's ice cubes are the amen that blesses a glass of water and turns it into a *drink*! They are also a kid- and adult-friendly way to liven up a glass of water. In my mother's novel *Ada's Rules*, one of Ada's ideas for losing weight is to treat herself to fancy ice cubes into which she has frozen various herbs. I think Dear inspired Ada.

12 fresh raspberries, blueberries, or clementine pieces

Put 1 piece of fruit in each compartment of a 12-slot ice cube tray, fill with water, and freeze until solid.

GRANDMA'S
BELLINI

MAKES 1 DRINK

Grandma Bontemps didn't drink often. She had grown up around too much wildness near the turpentine camps to be much intrigued by liquor, and when she came of age it was in a sober Seventh-day Adventist environment. Fortunately or unfortunately, after the Adventists tried to get Grandpa to burn his books when he was teaching at Oakwood College in Huntsville, it burned the Adventist right out of them. When I knew Grandma she was a Presbyterian. And she drank—but only Champagne, preferably muddled with a bit of Georgia or Alabama peach.

On one of Grandma's last birthdays, Mama and Godmommy Lea drove Grandma and her friends around Nashville in a limo, serving Bellinis and boxed lunches to the ladies. When Mama toasted Grandma, saying that Hemingway—for whom the drink was reportedly invented—wasn't the only great American writer to be drinking Bellinis, it was the first time Grandma's identity as poet was acknowledged in front of her clubwomen peers.

Our version of the Bellini harkens back to the very simple original. At clubwomen brunches we've encountered Bellinis made with peaches canned in heavy syrup, Bellinis that add a second alcohol to the Prosecco, usually peach schnapps or Grand Marnier, Bellinis that call for a single peach to be muddled with a half cup of sugar, Bellinis that call for orange juice, and many recipes that call for simple syrup. We know one lady who adds all of that and a little brandy to her Bellini! This Bellini is fresh fruit, Prosecco, and an eleven-calorie (per serving) taste of honey.

¼ ripe peach, peeled and chopped

½ teaspoon honey

¾ cup Prosecco or other dry sparkling wine, cold

Using a spoon, muddle the peach with the honey and pour into the bottom of a champagne flute. Top with the Prosecco and sip!

NOTE One 750 ml bottle of Prosecco, 1 peach, and 2 teaspoons of honey will make 4 Bellinis.

ONGOING STUDIES ARE EXPLORING THE HEALTH BENEFITS
of honey. In traditional African American folk medicine,
honey has been heralded as a cough suppressant, a cleans-
ing agent, and a cure for mouth sores. Today labs are exploring its antimicrobial and antiviral qualities. It's known that it
has trace antioxidants. Even though the jury is out on *proving*
honey is healthful, we like to honor the traditional black
medicinals. And we know that substituting honey for white
sugar has certain benefits: Honey has a glycemic index of 55
and white sugar has a glycemic index of 100. And because
you need to use less honey to achieve the same degree of
sweetness as when using white sugar, fewer calories go
into a serving when using honey. We can toast to all of that!

MAMA'S
TEQUILA ICE

MAKES 1 DRINK

Mama never drank much until she was well into her thirties. Newly out of college, sharing a group house in Washington, D.C., with three guy friends, she would drink a hot chocolate made with pure cream and real cocoa in a tiny demitasse while her roommates had an after-work cocktail, beer, or glass of wine. When she moved to Nashville to be a country songwriter at twenty-three, her workday began at 9 p.m., when the clubs opened. She vowed not to drink on the job, so she had coffee into the wee hours of the morning and sometimes found herself driving all her drunk friends home. Even after she married and had me, Mama hosted guitar pulls that lasted till morning; her only rule was that everybody had to be gone by the time I woke up at 7 a.m. and started looking for my breakfast. Then Mama was a single mama for about seven years before she married David and started drinking vodka tonics. We'll never know if it was age, the vodka, the sweet tonic, the stress of being married again, or the birth control shots, but the first year Mama was married she put on about forty pounds. And she kept putting on weight. Till she finally stopped. (Stopping gaining weight is the first often un-noted step before losing weight. I think it's the hardest step.)

One of the few fun and easy things for Mama when she started losing weight was exchanging vodka tonics and margaritas for straight tequila over ice. A vodka tonic can have about 160 calories, and a margarita, depending on size, more than 400 calories. A shot of tequila over ice? About 100. And when sipped instead of guzzled, tequila has a bright, exotic flavor. You can still get a buzz without all the pudge.

1 slice of lime

2 fingers of tequila (our very favorite is Clase Azul Reposado)

Fill a rocks glass or old-fashioned glass halfway with water and freeze until solid. Squeeze the lime over the ice, add the tequila, brace yourself, and sip!

CAROLINE'S
HOTTY TODDY

MAKES 1 DRINK

When you live on the Square in Oxford, Mississippi, whether or not you go to Ole Miss football games, you learn how to make a hot toddy. I live on the Square, I've bought more than one red dress to wear on game day, and I've put my own spin on the hotty toddy.

When I first moved to Mississippi, I lived in Greenwood. Hiram Eastland took me and a few other Teach for America teachers under his wing. Hiram has many claims to fame, from "going medieval on BP's ass" after the Gulf Coast oil spill to attending Ole Miss football games with James Meredith, the first African American to attend Ole Miss. Every game I go to, I drink my first hotty toddy to Meredith's health. I drink my second one in honor of William Faulkner. We've got a cookbook in our collection to which Faulkner contributed a hotty toddy recipe. He lived near the Square before I did.

A finger of brown liquor
  (see note)

1 teaspoon honey

1 teaspoon fresh lemon juice

1 cup strong spiced black tea,
  such as Constant Comment,
  hot

1 cinnamon stick

Combine the liquor, honey, and lemon juice in a mason jar, and add the hot tea. Stir well with a cinnamon stick, and then keep it in the jar. Enjoy!

NOTE Our favorite brown liquor is Jack Daniel's. We also love the high rye bourbon blends such as Four Roses, Woodford Reserve, and Bulleit. When considering wheat-based bourbons, we love opposite ends of the same street: Rebel Yell is our frugal favorite and Pappy Van Winkle is the splurge. When you're mixing up a toddy, stick with the great Tennessee whiskey, Jack Daniel's!

NANA'S
MARTINI

MAKES 1 DRINK

Nana loved her liquor. Anytime you saw her after noon, she was likely to have a glass in her hand. She liked scotch on ice if she was in the house, but if she was out she enjoyed a martini, preferably dry, with an interesting olive in a pretty stemmed glass. She would have found this martini quite acceptable.

2 fingers of vodka, cold

1 tiny whole pickled green tomato

Pour the vodka into a mason jar, add ice cubes, and screw the lid on tight. Shake hard for 15 seconds. Strain into a martini glass, using the lid to hold back the ice. Drop in the pickled green tomato, and enjoy.

GEORGE WASHINGTON CARVER CALLED PICKLED GREEN tomatoes "Vermont olives." You can find them in many grocery stores (they are often called "tomolives"), or you can make your own using Carver's recipe but substituting cherry tomatoes for the plum or fig tomatoes he calls for:

"Take a bushel of green and half-ripe tomatoes (the plum or fig tomatoes are preferable); wash clean; pack in big jar or tub; use 5 lbs. fine salt, ½ lb. whole mixed spices; weight down and cover with cold clear water. In two weeks they are fit to use, and will keep for months if kept under the pickle. They are used without further fixing."

PEPPER JELLY
COINS

Nana often made pepper jelly. Some years she made bright green and bright red jars of it to give away as Christmas gifts. Much more often she would pour a jar of homemade pepper jelly over cream cheese and serve it with Triscuits. Pepper jelly coins are more fun to make and are quietly dramatic. We invented them one day when John Egerton, author of *Southern Food* and one of the founding fathers of the Southern Foodways Alliance, was coming to supper. They made him smile. Nowadays most folks know Egerton, who died while we were working on this book, as a foodie. My family knew him first as a fine soldier in the civil rights movement. When big Avon died, John gave the eulogy. At the dinner where these coins were first served, John agreed that Southerners as a group are most proud of our food and our music. And we're most ashamed of our politics and our economics.

1 packet (1.75 ounces) fruit pectin

5 cups sugar

4 red bell peppers, chopped, with seeds

2 orange bell peppers, chopped, with seeds

2 yellow bell peppers, chopped, with seeds

2 fresh red chile peppers, seeded and chopped

¾ cup apple cider vinegar

14 to 20 slices of thin-sliced white sandwich bread

1 Mix the pectin with ½ cup of the sugar and set off to the side.

2 Bring the peppers, vinegar, and the remaining sugar to a vigorous simmer in a nonreactive saucepan. Cook for 10 minutes over medium heat, stirring steadily to prevent scorching or burning. Add the pectin mixture and increase the heat to bring the mixture to a full boil (what Mama likes to call a "rolling boil," because big bubbles roll up to the surface). Keep the mixture at a full boil for a minute, still stirring. When it's ready, the jelly should thickly coat a metal spoon dipped into the pan. When you've got that happening, set your peppers aside to cool in the pan. Once cool, pepper jelly should glump up on a spoon just like grape jelly. Pour into pint jars and refrigerate for up to a month.

NOTE You can make three subtly different colored pepper jellies— red, orange, and yellow—using all of one color pepper in three separate batches. In one batch put 1½ hot peppers, in another just ½ hot pepper, and in the final batch none. If you put three coins, one of each color, on a small plate and garnish it with fresh chives, you have a very pretty appetizer.

3 To make the base for your coins, on a clean flat surface covered in foil or wax paper, use a rolling pin to roll a single piece of bread till very, very, very thin. Stamp 2 or 3 coins out of each piece of bread using a 1-inch cutter or, as Mama does, a champagne flute. Repeat until you have 40 bread coins.

4 Spread each bread coin with pepper jelly, and serve.

SOUTHERN
HUMMUS

MAKES 2 CUPS

I grew up with hummus in the house. Homemade hummus and store-bought hummus. The first "dinner" I ever remember making for myself by myself was probably a hummus plate. Cooking involved nothing more than splitting a pocket pita in half, cutting both halves into triangles, toasting them under the broiler, and arranging them on the plate with hummus spooned from a plastic tub. I still love that meal. Only now I love to make my own hummus, which is not much harder than spooning from a tub. Homemade hummus is a one-button small kitchen miracle.

We like to replace the traditional sesame paste with peanut butter. It's cheaper, more readily available, and far more Southern. We've also experimented with making a wide variety of hummuses from a variety of beans beyond the chickpea and the black-eyed pea. You can make a great hummus with lima beans or white beans. While we always used to serve this with pita triangles, we now gravitate toward carrot sticks and cucumber slices.

½ cup natural peanut butter

½ cup fresh lemon juice

1 garlic clove

1 (15-ounce) can chickpeas, rinsed and drained

½ cup warm water

1 teaspoon ground cumin

Salt and pepper

2 tablespoons extra virgin olive oil

I have made this in a blender and in a food processor. The food processor is slightly easier, but the blender works. Put the peanut butter, lemon juice, and garlic in your blender or food processor and whirl until the garlic vanishes into the peanut butter. Next add the chickpeas, warm water, and cumin, season with salt and pepper, and whirl a bit more. Finally, add the olive oil and whirl until smooth. Transfer to a bowl and serve.

BLACK-EYED PEA
HUMMUS

MAKES 2 CUPS

From Emily Morgan, the real Yellow Rose of Texas and a woman of color, to Britt Johnson, a nineteenth-century black teamster who went alone on a yearlong horseback journey into the Comancheria to find and rescue his black wife, to all manner of black cowboys, Texas has given America more than its share of black heroes—and we have long been fascinated by audacious black Texans who just don't do stuff like other folks do.

In the Lone Star State they make something called "Texas caviar," which is black-eyed pea salad, often served on corn chips as an appetizer. The individual peas look like giant or Texas-size caviar eggs, and the salad frequently appears on the menus at Links functions in the great state of Texas. Necessity inspired our creation of black-eyed pea hummus. Years ago, finding myself with no chickpeas or tahini and hungry for hummus, I reached for the black-eyed peas and peanut butter in my pantry, and the combination worked.

1 (15-ounce) can black-eyed peas, rinsed and drained

4 garlic cloves

2 tablespoons natural peanut butter

1 tablespoon fresh lemon juice

½ teaspoon paprika

Salt and pepper

¼ cup extra virgin olive oil

Put the black-eyed peas and garlic in a food processor. Whirl until the garlic is finely chopped and relatively evenly distributed in the black-eyed peas. Add the peanut butter and whirl again until blended. Add the lemon juice and paprika, season with salt and pepper, and whirl until the mixture begins to form a relatively smooth paste. Slowly pour in the olive oil with the motor running. Keep whirling until smooth. Taste, and add more salt and pepper if necessary. We like a light hand on the salt and a heavy hand on the pepper.

RED SPREAD

MAKES 2 CUPS

In 1965, just after Lyndon Johnson got the Voting Rights Act passed by the Senate but before he could get it through the House, an international congress of writers organized by PEN met in Yugoslavia. My great-grandparents, Arna and Alberta Bontemps, were members of the PEN group, led by playwright Arthur Miller, who traveled to Europe. Alberta told the story of being entertained by President Tito with great pride and considerable humor. Her tale involved foreign dignitaries as well as gastric distress. This didn't stop her from recounting her memories of *ajvar*, a delicious red pepper spread, one of the few Yugoslavian dishes she could re-create in her kitchen. Twenty-plus years later, Mama travelled to Yugoslavia with her college roommate Mimi, who became my godmother, and fell in love with *ajvar* all over again. It's a fine dip that, unlike so many Southern spreads, does not rely on sour cream or mayonnaise. We love to serve red spread on raw red pepper strips. It's also great on raw cucumber slices.

4 large red bell peppers

1 medium eggplant

3 garlic cloves

½ cup olive oil

Salt and pepper

1 Preheat the broiler.

2 First, roast the red peppers (see page 98). Leave them to cool while you prepare the eggplant.

3 Prick the eggplant all over with a fork. Broil it until it is blistered all over. Remove from the broiler and set on a cutting board to cool. While the eggplant is cooling, peel and seed the cooled peppers. Then peel the eggplant.

4 In a food processor combine the red pepper, eggplant, and garlic, and whirl until the mixture begins to become smooth. Slowly add the olive oil with the motor running. Whirl until completely smooth. Season with salt and pepper to taste. Use immediately or refrigerate in a glass jar for up to several adays.

HOMEMADE SALSA
WITH CUCUMBER CHIPS

MAKES 5 CUPS

African American foodways are constantly evolving. One of the strongest current influences on the evolution is increasing encounters with Hispanic culture as Latinos become the largest minority group in the United States. One of the many positive developments? Salsa has overtaken corn-syrup-laden ketchup as the number-one-selling condiment.

The world's largest salsa festival takes place in Oxnard, California, and features a variety of salsa cooking contests that underscore the different styles and complexities of this now ubiquitous dish. The private chef of actor and producer Will Smith recently took first prize in the People's Choice and Best Hot Salsa categories: Ross Ruiz's recipe included mangoes as well as tomatoes. Our salsa is more back to basics, and is an easy replacement for the store-bought variety.

Salsa is an excellent way to start a meal—especially when you replace the fried tortilla chips with cucumber slices! I love to keep a bowl of this in the refrigerator to pull out for unexpected company. And salsa is our go-to substitute for salad dressing; just drizzle with a little olive oil and you're good to go.

5 medium tomatoes

3 serrano chiles

1 jalapeño

¼ cup chopped white onion

½ cup chopped green onion (white and green parts)

⅓ cup chopped fresh cilantro

½ teaspoon salt

½ teaspoon dried oregano

1 tablespoon extra virgin olive oil

2 garlic cloves

3 cucumbers, rinsed

1 Whirl 2 or 3 tomatoes at a time in a food processor until they reach your preferred salsa consistency, and then pour into a nonreactive bowl. Whirl the serrano chiles, jalapeño, white onion, green onion, cilantro, salt, oregano, olive oil, and garlic in the food processor until chopped super-fine. Stir into the tomatoes. Cover with plastic wrap, refrigerate, and let the flavors meld for at least 30 minutes and up to overnight.

2 Slice the cucumbers into "chips" that are thick enough to stand up to a heap of salsa. Serve the salsa with the cucumber slices for dipping.

BABA GHANOUSH

MAKES 5 CUPS

"The Cumberland is a river in the Middle East." That's a line from Mama's novel *Rebel Yell,* about a black spy family. It's also the truth. Nashville has a very large Kurdish population, the largest of any city in the United States. The Kurd migration to middle Tennessee began about the time Mama moved to the city in 1983. For a very long time the primary ethnic food you could find in Nashville wasn't Chinese, or Japanese, or even Mexican; it was Middle Eastern. Growing up in Washington, D.C., Mama had tasted Middle Eastern food; her very best friend's mother was Israeli, and though that family served European haute cuisine, when Mama pictured Leslie's summer days in Tel Aviv she imagined her munching on olives and hummus and baba ghanoush, which Mama tried to re-create in her blender. In fact, hummus and baba ghanoush were some of the first foods Mama turned to when seeking a different kind of kitchen for her daughter than she had had for herself.

These days, I'm team hummus, and Mama is team baba ghanoush, but this recipe is good enough to make me a fair-weather fan. To get the flavor of the cumin and paprika what I like to think of as loud and fully bloomed, we cook the eggplant a little differently in this recipe than I do when cooking Red Spread.

3 large eggplants

Salt

3 tablespoons extra virgin olive oil

1/8 teaspoon ground cumin

1/8 teaspoon smoked paprika

1/3 cup natural peanut butter

Juice of 3 lemons

Pepper

3 tablespoons chopped fresh herbs, such as a mix of parsley, mint, and cilantro

1 Preheat the oven to 450°F.

2 Prick the skin of the eggplants all over with a fork. Slice the eggplants in half lengthwise, and put them, skin side down, on a foil-lined baking sheet. Sprinkle the eggplant halves with salt, drizzle with the olive oil, and then sprinkle the cumin and smoked paprika over the top. Roast until the eggplant is soft, about 30 minutes.

3 Remove the eggplants from the oven, and let them cool long enough so that you are able to safely touch them. Scoop the meat out of the eggplants and drop it into a food processor or blender. Add the peanut butter, lemon juice, and 3 tablespoons of water. Whirl until smooth. Season with salt and pepper to taste. Scoop into a bowl and sprinkle with the herbs before serving.

ROASTED PEPPERS
WITH SARDINES AND BOILED EGGS

SERVES 6 TO 8

Roasted peppers are a favorite thing I inherited from Mama; they were a staple in her kitchen. I love their rich, smoky flavor and beautiful color. We like to serve them with sardines and hard-boiled eggs to make a party platter.

We think it's time to move sardines out of the shadows of Motown. They are cheap, delicious, and quick. They are also packed with nutrients, low in calories, and a highly sustainable food source. Sardines are a perfect *now food* that we abandoned after it became associated with being black and poor. Christopher Smalls, better known to the world as the late, great Notorious B.I.G., took a jab at the small fish in his hit "Juicy." Reflecting upon his days of poverty, he rapped, "Remember when I used to eat sardines for dinner." To him, they were a hardship. But when I think about how they are at the core of what helps people get by when they've got nothing else to hold them up, I think they are a hallelujah.

Finally, it doesn't get more basic or old-school than hard-boiled eggs. Because they are easy to tote and relatively neat to eat, hard-boiled eggs wrapped in tinfoil were staple foods on long train or car rides and in segregated colored classrooms throughout the first half of the twentieth century. They were also frequently served at bars. The week after Easter, they were usually on the daily breakfast menu as children tried to make their way through their Easter baskets. Hard-boiled eggs cover a lot of territory.

As a trio, these simple ingredients make a beautiful, healthy, tasty alternative to the classic cold-cuts-and-cheese combo.

6 bell peppers, preferably a mix of red, orange, and yellow

½ cup olive oil

Salt and pepper

2 (3.75-ounce) cans sardines, drained

½ lemon

6 hard-boiled eggs

1 Preheat the broiler.

2 Put the peppers on the top rack of the oven, directly under the broiler. Allow the skins of the peppers to blister. When they have blistered on one side, turn them to another, using tongs and being careful not to burn your hand! When the peppers are blistered on all sides, remove them from the broiler, put them directly in a clean brown paper or a plastic bag, and close the bag. Allow the peppers to steam,

NOTE To hard-boil eggs, bring a medium saucepan of water to a boil. Carefully add the eggs and boil for 8 minutes. Drain, and plunge the eggs into an ice bath to cool.

then rest, in the bag until the bag is cool. This may take about 30 minutes. Open the bag.

3 Slice off the tops of the peppers, peel off the skins, and cut out the ribs and seeds. Slice the skinless pepper flesh into ½-inch-wide strips, transfer them to a platter, and douse with the olive oil. Season with salt and pepper to taste. (Suspended in olive oil, these peppers will last 2 or 3 days in the fridge.)

4 Arrange the sardines next to the peppers. Squeeze the lemon half over the sardines. Dust with a grating of black pepper. Peel and halve the eggs, and nestle them on the platter. Sprinkle the eggs with salt and pepper.

GUACAMOLE

MAKES 4 CUPS

This bright green spread is known as a "freedom food" in our family. Arna first ate it in California when he was growing up. Joan frequently served it as part of her bar-food repertoire. I perfected my version of guacamole in England while trying out American favorites on my English friends.

Mama vividly remembers the day she learned to make guacamole, taught to her by a northern Californian, a freshman-year friend. They were in the grocery store, picking out avocados, when Mama told her friend, who was visiting during a school break, that she was being abused by a relative, the very relative they were cooking for that night. As they chopped avocados and tomatoes, they planned to confront the relative over dinner.

Emboldened by the presence of her friend and a taste of summer in the middle of winter, Mama found her voice. The relative never abused her again, and we've been eating guacamole with a particular pleasure ever since.

3 large ripe avocados, pitted

1 small red onion, finely chopped

1 small sweet yellow onion, finely chopped

¼ cup chopped fresh cilantro

2 jalapeños, seeded and chopped

Juice of 2 limes

¼ teaspoon ground cumin

1 medium tomato, diced

Salt and pepper

Scoop the flesh from the avocados into a bowl. Add the red and yellow onions, cilantro, jalapeños, lime juice, and cumin, and mash the mixture together with a fork. Mix in the tomatoes and season with salt and pepper to taste. Be careful not to over-mash! You want the avocado to keep a little texture.

GEORGE WASHINGTON CARVER'S
HOMEMADE PEANUT BUTTER

MAKES 4 CUPS

There are competing ideas about who invented peanut butter, but everyone knows who popularized it in twentieth-century black America: George Washington Carver. Fresh peanut butter with no added sugar is a protein-rich, creamy delicacy that you can whirl up in a blender. Once you've got the basics down, you can add various spices, such as cinnamon or cayenne or Chinese five-spice powder—be creative! Peanut butter is a bass note that can carry a wide variety of top notes.

8 cups roasted unsalted
  peanuts
4 tablespoons peanut oil
½ tablespoon salt

Put 1 cup of the peanuts in a food processor or blender with 1 tablespoon of the peanut oil. Whirl until chunky. Add the rest of the peanuts, cup by cup, whirling a teaspoon or so of peanut oil in after each cup, until the peanut butter starts to become smooth. Add the salt and continue whirling. Use the remaining peanut oil as needed to help the peanut butter develop a smooth texture.

SOUPS

SWEET POTATO BROTH

CHICKEN BROTH

GREEN BROTH

BROCCOLI SOUP

ASPARAGUS SOUP

CARROT GINGER SOUP

AFRICAN CHICKPEA SOUP

COLD CUCUMBER SOUP

SWEET POTATO
BROTH

One January a few years back, Mama needed a quick substitute for chicken stock. The author Randall Kenan was coming for dinner. On the menu was a New South classic: black-eyed pea and kale stew made with homemade chicken broth. But just before Mama began to stir up a pot of worthy tribute to a writer who has made small-town black North Carolina a place readers of all colors wish to linger, we got a call alerting us that another dinner guest was a vegetarian. Fortunately, the ghost of George Washington Carver, perhaps inspired by Kenan's first novel, *A Visitation of Spirits,* entered our kitchen and started tugging on an apron. Mama called me to throw around ideas for alternative stocks. Before we knew it, we were inventing— just like Carver. (And changing that stew forever; see page 143 for the recipe.)

This sweet potato broth is easy, delicious, cheap, and vegetarian—and it isn't salty. Canned chicken stocks, while convenient, often have way too much salt. And the flavors can be tinny, flat, or just plain off.

I also love this broth because the recipe is not meant to be exact. You can't mess it up, and you don't get more Southern than a sweet potato. Improvise with what you have on hand and with what your taste buds tell you ought to happen.

1 medium onion, sliced

3 celery stalks, chopped

1 carrot, chopped

Olive oil

1 large sweet potato

5 whole cloves

Salt and pepper

1 In a large stockpot, sauté the onion, celery, and carrot in a tablespoon or so of olive oil—just enough to cover the bottom of your pot—over low heat. Meanwhile, peel and quarter the sweet potato. When the onion has softened, after about 8 minutes, add the sweet potato to the pot along with 6 cups of water, the cloves, and a little salt and pepper. Bring to a boil, then lower the heat and simmer until the sweet potato is completely soft, about 30 minutes.

2 Fish out the cloves, then puree the mixture in a blender or food processor, or if you're working without fancy tools, by mashing the sweet potato into the side of the pot with a wooden spoon and stirring. If not using immediately, let cool, then cover and refrigerate for up to 5 days or freeze for up to 2 months.

CHICKEN
BROTH

MAKES 3 QUARTS

I usually make this after I've roasted a chicken and picked it to the bone. But if I leave a little meat on the bone, the stock is so much the better. And if I make this with the carcass from my Spicy Pepper Chicken (page 122) instead of my Chicken Roasted with Lemon and Onion (page 118), well, the stock has just that much more kick.

5 medium carrots

5 celery stalks

1 onion

1 garlic clove

Carcass of a roasted chicken

1 teaspoon salt

6 whole cloves

1 sprig fresh rosemary

5 sprigs fresh thyme

4 bay leaves

1 Roughly chop all the carrots, celery, and onion. Throw them in a great big pot, and add the garlic, chicken carcass, salt, cloves, rosemary, thyme, and bay leaves. Pour in 4 quarts of water and bring to a rolling boil. Reduce the heat to medium and simmer, stirring occasionally, for 3 hours.

2 Strain the liquid and let it cool (discard the solids). Cover and refrigerate for up to 5 days or freeze in 1-cup portions for easy use for up to several months.

GREEN
BROTH

MAKES 2 QUARTS

Gol-ly. Green broth was the one recipe in this book we really had to think about for a spell. Because the thing is, you can't always count on a green vegetable being boiled into a broth to hold its color, can you? And a golden or orange broth can turn many green soups into a funky-colored mess. This vegetarian broth adds not only flavor but also great color to soups.

1 bunch green onions (white and green parts)

2 large onions

1 bunch fresh parsley

2 tablespoons olive oil

6 garlic cloves

½ tablespoon salt

4 bay leaves

3 cups fresh watercress

1 Roughly chop the green onions, onions, and parsley. Heat the olive oil in a large pot over medium heat. Add the green onions, onions, parsley, and garlic, and cook for 5 minutes. Add 6 cups of water, the salt, and the bay leaves, and bring to a boil. Cover, lower the heat, and simmer for 1 hour.

2 Strain the liquid, discarding the solids, and pour it into a blender. Add the watercress and whirl until smooth.

NOTES You can add cilantro and a jalapeño, or basil and red pepper flakes, to this broth. For a green broth with a sweeter flavor, substitute fresh mint for half the watercress.

BROCCOLI
SOUP

SERVES 8

Born and raised in the South, I have sipped my share of broccoli soups—primarily cream, or cheese, or cream and cheese, with a little broccoli thrown in there for texture. This soup is different. Using our Green Broth as a base, we are able to pass on the cheese and cream and still achieve a rich-tasting result. Plus, our soup is cheaper than many classic broccoli soups.

1 medium yellow onion

2 garlic cloves

2 tablespoons olive oil

2 large heads broccoli, roughly chopped

2 quarts Green Broth (opposite)

1 tablespoon ground nutmeg

½ teaspoon cayenne pepper

Salt

1 Roughly chop the onion and garlic. Cook the olive oil in a large pot over medium heat until the onion begins to soften, about 5 minutes. Add the broccoli and continue to cook for another 5 minutes. Pour in the broth and bring to a boil. Add the nutmeg and cayenne. Reduce the heat and simmer until the broccoli is just done and still green, about 5 minutes.

2 Remove from the heat, and whirl the entire mixture in a food processor or blender until smooth. Return the soup to the pot and bring to a simmer. Taste, add salt if needed, and then serve.

NOTE We like to garnish this verdant soup with a dollop of Greek yogurt, fresh herbs, a grating of Parmesan, or croutons. Sometimes we fish out a few nice broccoli florets from the pot before pureeing and add them to each bowl as garnish.

ASPARAGUS
SOUP

This soup is what I like to call "fancy"—as the Drake song says, "Nails done, hair done, everything did / Oh, you fancy, huh?" Fancy. Asparagus just got it like that. Their flavor is naturally complex, earthy and sweet at the same time. And did I say beautiful? An asparagus spear is a thing of beauty and wholly edible raw. Blended into a green soup, asparagus makes a perfect start to a meal—or its own meal when rounded out with bread and cheese. And you can fancy up the fancy by garnishing your bowl with an elegant green asparagus tip.

3 pounds asparagus

1 white onion

1½ quarts Green Broth (page 106)

1 teaspoon salt

1 teaspoon white pepper

1 cup fat-free sour cream

1 Cut the bottom inch off of the asparagus stalks and discard. Cut 6 to 8 tips off individual spears and save the tips for garnish. Chop up the remaining asparagus and the onion, and put in a large pot. Pour in the broth, and add the salt and white pepper. Bring to a boil over high heat. Then reduce the heat and simmer, covered, until the asparagus is soft, 5 to 10 minutes.

2 Pour the mixture into a blender or food processor and whirl until smooth. Add the sour cream, and continue whirling until combined. Return the soup to the pot, bring to a simmer, and then serve.

NOTE This soup is also lovely served cold.

CARROT GINGER
SOUP

SERVES 8

The first time I remember making this soup, I was cooking with Mama for our mother-daughter book club. I was about ten. We'd read *Ella Enchanted,* a book that ultimately inspired Mama and me to share with a larger world the black fairy-tale princess, B.B. Bright, we had begun creating when I was very small. Carrot ginger soup is the kind of thing the heroine of *The Diary of B.B. Bright, Possible Princess* would eat. It makes me want to shout out with gratitude to Shireen Dodson, the African American mother who wrote *The Mother-Daughter Book Club* and inspired us to start a book club of our own. (It is wild to imagine that some mother-daughter pair somewhere may read *this* book in their meeting.) Most recently, I made this soup at Easter along with Roasted Leg of Lamb (page 207). This soup has an amazing color, and is a perfect addition to any celebration table.

2 large yellow onions, chopped

¼ cup grated peeled fresh ginger

2 tablespoons olive oil

4 pounds carrots, roughly chopped

1½ quarts Chicken Broth (page 105)

1 teaspoon grated lemon zest

½ tablespoon salt

1 In a large pot, cook the onions and ginger in the olive oil over medium heat until the onions soften, about 5 minutes. Add the carrots, broth, lemon zest, and salt, and simmer until the carrots are soft enough to pierce easily with a fork, about 25 minutes.

2 Pour the contents of the pot into a blender or food processor, and whirl until smooth. Return the soup to the pot, bring to a simmer, and then serve.

AFRICAN CHICKPEA
SOUP

SERVES 8

The first people in our family to get involved with genealogy were Uncle Paul and Aunt Sonia Bontemps. Paul was the oldest son of the Bontemps family, his birth following so closely after Joan's that Grandma referred to the siblings as "Irish twins." Paul and Sonia's wedding was considered the finest event the family ever threw; the details were discussed for decades. Aunt Sonia was a doctor's daughter and only child. With the help of her parents, Uncle Paul and Aunt Sonia purchased a large modern house near Artichoke Reservoir in Newburyport, Massachusetts.

As the years went by, Sonia and Paul developed a passionate interest in genealogy, helping to found an African American genealogical society and taking Grandma on a trip to revisit the scenes of her youth. They went through all the family stories, taking time to separate the fact from the fiction. One of the myths they explored but could not prove was that the Bontemps family had a connection to Madagascar. Whether or not this is true (how many descendants of slaves can really know their exact African origins?), the thought encouraged us to explore Madagascan foodstuffs and foodways, culminating in this hearty and healthy recipe. Many chickpea soups have evolved from North Africa; this one features coconut milk, a Madagascar signature.

8 cups mustard greens

2 garlic cloves, chopped

1 tablespoon olive oil

1 teaspoon crushed red pepper flakes

1 teaspoon ground coriander

¼ teaspoon ground cardamom

½ teaspoon cayenne pepper

Pinch of ground turmeric

1 quart Sweet Potato Broth (page 104)

Wash the mustard greens well—you want to get all the dirt off. You can rinse them leaf by leaf under running water, or soak a bunch in a large bowl of cold water, swishing with your hands. Some people like to make a ritual of this, insisting on seven changes of cold water, one for each day of the week. They use the process of cooking greens to remember the Creation story. In our experience three or four changes of clean cold water will usually do the trick, but the point to remember is this: as long as you find some dirt in the bottom of the bowl, you need another change of water. Once the greens are clean, roll them up loosely and then chop the rolls. The size of the pieces you prefer to have in your soup will determine how you chop. If you want smaller greens pieces in your soup, chop the roll lengthwise and sideways.

1 cup unsweetened coconut
    milk

2 (16-ounce) cans chickpeas,
    rinsed and drained

Salt and pepper

2 Cook the garlic in the olive oil in a large pot over medium
    heat for about 1 minute. Then add the pepper flakes,
coriander, cardamom, cayenne, and turmeric. Cook for another
minute or two. (Toasting the spices opens up their flavor.)
Add the greens, sweet potato broth, and coconut milk. Bring
to a gentle boil, then add the chickpeas. Lower the heat and
simmer until the greens are nice and soft, about 1½ hours.

3 Season to taste with salt and pepper before ladling into
    bowls.

COLD CUCUMBER
SOUP

SERVES 8

Cucumber soups appear in many African American community cookbooks and in many early Southern cookbooks—which is not surprising, as cucumbers were often available, cheap to buy, and easy to grow. Nowadays, those soups are often forgotten, and all that remains to remind us of the cucumbers that used to grow in black gardens are pickles. I mean, just think, you can still buy a pickle in a plastic wrapper for about a dollar at most convenience stores and gas stations in the Mississippi Delta. And pickles were easily the healthiest thing for sale when I worked the football game concession stand at Ruleville Central High School.

In my Mississippi kitchen I've combined elements of old-fashioned cucumber soup and white gazpacho (a Spanish dish made with almonds, grapes, bread, and cucumbers) to create a refreshing chunky soup that's perfect for summer porch parties. It can be portioned into small mason jars that double as serving bowls and refrigerated until serving time.

2 celery stalks (including the leaves), chopped

2 small green bell peppers, seeded and chopped

5 cucumbers, peeled and chopped

1 fresh chile, such as jalapeño or serrano, chopped

4 garlic cloves

12 fresh basil leaves

¼ cup fresh parsley leaves, chopped

3 tablespoons white wine vinegar

½ cup olive oil

1 cup plain yogurt

Salt and white pepper

1 Mix the celery, bell peppers, cucumbers, and chile together in a large bowl.

2 Whirl the garlic cloves, basil, parsley, vinegar, olive oil, and 2 cups of water together in a blender or food processor until the greens are finely chopped and equally distributed in the liquid. Add 2 cups of ice cubes and the yogurt, and whirl to the consistency of a frosty. Pour this spiked oil-and-vinegar dressing over your chopped vegetables and stir. Add salt and white pepper to taste, noting that cold soups take a tiny bit more salt than hot soups.

MAIN DISHES

POULTRY

CHICKEN ROASTED WITH LEMON AND ONION

STEAMED CHICKEN AND BROCCOLI WITH BASIL

CHICKEN BREASTS WITH GRAPES AND MUSHROOMS

SPICY PEPPER CHICKEN

PEANUT CHICKEN STEW

CHICKEN, VEGETABLE, AND WILD RICE STEW

TURKEY BURGERS

FISH

JOAN'S NIÇOISE WITH OKRA LADYFINGERS

COUNTEE AND YOLANDE'S POACHED SALMON WITH LEEKS

SHRIMP STEW

SALMON CROQUETTES WITH DILL SAUCE

SHRIMP SALAD

GEORGE'S RED SNAPPER

BEANS

RED AND BLACK BEAN BURGERS

SWEET POTATO, KALE, AND BLACK-EYED PEA SOUP

RED BEAN AND BROWN RICE CREOLE SALAD

OAKWOOD BEAN LOAF

POET'S POT PIE

CHICKEN ROASTED
WITH LEMON AND ONION

SERVES 4 TO 5

If there is one dish that epitomizes my kitchen now, it is this one. I started cooking this when I was studying in England, but African Americans have been eating chicken, significantly, for a very long time. People have built houses out of chicken legs by frying them up and selling them; Psyche Williams-Forson wrote a powerful book about it, *Building Houses out of Chicken Legs*. Women have honored the community preachers by cooking him their most succulent hens. In my family a hen was what Dear served from the pot every Sunday, God sent. When I eat chicken, I taste my past and the triumph of my foremothers. This chicken is roasted, not fried. Fried chicken is a bad boyfriend. Time to kick that so-and-so out of the house.

1 (3- to 4-pound) chicken

Salt and pepper

2 medium yellow onions, halved

2 lemons, thinly sliced

6 sprigs fresh rosemary, or
  2 tablespoons dried

⅓ cup olive oil

1 Preheat the oven to 400°F.

2 Remove the giblets, neck, and liver packet—anything stuffed in the interior of the chicken. Rinse the chicken inside and out, and pat dry. Put the chicken in a baking dish with low sides. Season generously with salt and pepper inside and out. Put one onion half, a quarter of the lemon slices, and 2 of the rosemary sprigs (or 2 teaspoons of the dried rosemary) inside the chicken cavity. Rub the olive oil all over the outside of the bird. Quarter the remaining onion halves and spread them, together with the remaining lemon slices, evenly over the chicken. Scatter the remaining 4 rosemary sprigs (or 4 teaspoons dried rosemary) over the chicken.

3 Roast the chicken until it reaches an internal temperature of 160°F; the juices should run clear and colorless, not even a little bit pink, when you pierce a thigh. This can take 45 minutes to 1 hour.

4 Remove the dish from the oven and let the chicken rest for 15 minutes before carving and serving.

STEAMED CHICKEN
AND BROCCOLI WITH BASIL

SERVES 4

This is the very first dish I cooked with goods from Walmart when I was teaching first grade in a town called Moorhead in the Mississippi Delta. The Southern train line crosses the Yellow Dog train line in Moorhead, which makes it one of only a few places with a legitimate claim to the title "Birthplace of the Blues." Folks in Moorhead know their town *is the place,* and you know what? I believe them. The Delta is a land of beauty and difficulty, a place of trauma and transcendence. It's where Fannie Lou Hamer said, "I'm sick and tired of being sick and tired," and the place where they beat her in the courthouse jail for trying to vote and trying to take care of herself. It's where bluesman Robert Johnson imagined a hell more frightening than Dante's. As fog rose from the catfish ponds, I drove to school down the same road where Emmet Till was dragged to his death. Some mornings I would cry—it was that beautiful and that sad. Some mornings I called Mama and we talked all the way to my schoolhouse door, where I tried to undo just a little of the damage done by Jim Crow and the Cotton Kings. When I got home those days, I needed something to eat that was clean, uncomplicated, and homemade. Something that would do me no more harm, that wouldn't be so hard. This dish might seem plain, but it was my fast food, and it got me through the hard parts of my Delta days. When I told Mama about this recipe, she adopted it, and it started getting her through her hard days, too.

¼ cup loosely packed fresh
   basil leaves

4 boneless, skinless chicken
   breasts (each about 6 ounces)

Salt and pepper

1 lemon, thinly sliced

4 stalks broccoli, trimmed

1 Suspend a colander over a large pot that's halfway filled with water. (The water should not touch the colander.) Line the colander with half of the basil leaves, and add the chicken breasts in an even layer. Season the chicken with salt and pepper and then cover the chicken with half of the lemon slices. Put the pot over high heat and bring the water to a boil. Cover and steam for 15 minutes.

2 Add the broccoli to the colander and steam until the chicken is cooked through and the broccoli is tender, 10 minutes. Serve with the remaining lemon slices and basil.

CHICKEN BREASTS
WITH GRAPES AND MUSHROOMS

SERVES 4

This is a dish Mama didn't teach me to make until we were writing this cookbook. She had cooked it so many times before I was born and when I was little that by the time I was old enough to start cooking, I assumed she was tired of it. That was only part of the story.

In truth, she didn't want me to cook the dish especially for her. One of the Lutheran Lady's (her mother's) lesser sins was that she used her only daughter as a domestic servant. In Mama's high school days, Suprême de Volaille Véronique, aka Chicken Breasts with Grapes and Mushrooms, was a dish she had cooked time after time and often under duress.

Recognizing that the cooking we're doing is about a new kind of survival skills, I decided to take this dish out of retirement. I cook it, for my mama, with free will and pleasure. And I cook it to honor every woman who was ever "the help" in someone else's home or her own.

1 medium onion, chopped

2 cups button mushrooms, stemmed

1 tablespoon butter

2 cups seedless grapes

2 tablespoons dried tarragon

¼ cup heavy cream

Olive oil

4 boneless, skinless chicken breasts (each about 6 ounces)

Salt and pepper

1 cup dry white wine

1 Preheat the oven to 375°F.

2 Sauté the onion and mushrooms in the butter in a medium sauté pan over medium heat for about 5 minutes. Add the grapes and tarragon, and cook until the onion is translucent, another 5 minutes. Add the cream and remove from the heat.

3 In a separate sauté pan, pour in enough olive oil to slick the pan and heat over high heat. Season the chicken on both sides with salt and pepper and sear in the pan until golden brown on both sides, about 4 minutes per side. Put the chicken breasts in a baking dish. Pour the wine into the pan that you used to sear the chicken, and heat it over medium heat. Using a spatula or a wooden spoon, gather up all the leavings from the chicken into the warm wine. Pour the wine over the chicken and top with the mushroom mixture. Cover, and bake until the chicken is cooked through, about 25 minutes.

4 Serve the chicken breasts smothered with the onion mixture.

SPICY PEPPER
CHICKEN

Nashville is famous for its "Hot Chicken." I like to get mine from Prince's Hot Chicken Shack. It's crispy on the outside and juicy on the inside, and it comes decorated with a thin round of bright green pickle that calls to mind a gold medal. Prince's chicken is so hot, it can make a body see things. Speak in tongues. Change lives. This chicken is also fried. Now, I've already told you what I think about regular fried chicken—that it's a bad boyfriend you've just got to give up.

But this hot chicken here? You can eat my Spicy Pepper Chicken whenever you like, and it's a friend you'll want to keep around. You feel me?

2 tablespoons cayenne pepper

⅓ cup olive oil

3 garlic cloves, minced

Salt

1 (3- to 4-pound) chicken

Pepper

1 Preheat the oven to 450°F.

2 Mix the cayenne, olive oil, garlic, and ½ teaspoon salt in a small bowl.

3 Remove the giblets, neck, and liver packet—anything stuffed in the interior of the chicken. Rinse the chicken inside and out, and pat dry. Put the chicken in a baking dish with low sides. Season it generously with salt and pepper inside and out. Starting at the neck of the chicken, and making sure to break no more of the skin than you have to, brush the oil mixture onto the chicken flesh, including the legs. The whole chicken should appear reddish.

4 Roast the chicken for 20 minutes to crisp the skin, then turn the heat down to 400°F. Continue to roast the chicken until it reaches an internal temperature of 160°F. The juices should run clear and colorless when you pierce a thigh. This can take another 25 to 40 minutes.

5 Remove the dish from the oven and let the chicken rest for 15 minutes before carving and serving.

PEANUT CHICKEN
STEW

We cannot always trust the written record. According to what was inked on paper, "20 and Odd" Africans arrived in Jamestown, Virginia, in August 1619. And this is the year usually given for the arrival of slaves in Virginia. It is now suspected that these were not the first Africans, only the first documented, and they were not precisely slaves.

So much remains undocumented. Flavors and food close some gaps. One of the most famous dishes from the early colonies is Virginia Peanut Soup. This is documented: Peanuts are indigenous to Peru. They traveled to Africa with Portuguese explorers, then traveled from Africa to North America with enslaved Africans.

West Africa, particularly Senegal and the Gambia, is known for peanut, or groundnut, stews. My mother often talks about how African all Americans are. This soup celebrates that reality. George and Martha Washington were known for their peanut soup. Wonder if they knew they were eating an African classic? The record doesn't tell.

A lot of times, when people say a soup is thick enough to be a meal, they're playing you. They might not mean to, but they are. This soup sustains.

3 cups chopped cooked chicken

1½ cups natural peanut butter

1 (28-ounce) can diced
  tomatoes, drained, or
  3½ cups diced fresh tomatoes

1 tablespoon curry powder

1 teaspoon cayenne pepper

1 quart Sweet Potato Broth
  (page 104)

Salt

½ cup chopped roasted
  unsalted peanuts

1 Put the chicken, peanut butter, tomatoes, curry powder, and cayenne in a medium pot and pour in the sweet potato broth. Season with salt to taste. Simmer over medium heat until the peanut butter is completely blended and the stew has a thick, even consistency, 20 minutes.

2 Ladle the stew into bowls and serve, sprinkling the chopped nuts over the top as a garnish.

CHICKEN, VEGETABLE, AND
WILD RICE STEW

SERVES 10 TO 12

This is a real-talk soul stew you can't get from a can. I ate it as a little girl, then revived it for my mama when she started eating in my kitchen. According to Mama, jumping into a bowl of this is like jumping onto Dear's lap. It's profoundly comforting. Thick with wild rice, it reminds us of the many foodways and foodstuffs Native Americans have contributed to the African American table. Cultivating wild rice is an important aspect of Native American culture in the Upper Midwest. The dish also plays homage to the idea many African Americans have that they are part Indian. Literary critic Henry Louis ("Skip") Gates, Jr., thinks this is largely a myth. I'm not so sure. Grandma believed she was part Indian. And my mama suspects that she's part Indian. What's for sure is that wild rice, like oats and quinoa, is a vegan source of protein.

Salt

2 cups wild rice

2 tablespoons butter

3 cups chopped carrots

3 cups chopped celery

8 cups Chicken Broth (page 105)

10 sprigs fresh thyme

Pepper

3 cups shredded cooked chicken

1 Bring 6 cups of water to a boil in a medium saucepan. Season with ½ teaspoon salt and add the wild rice. Bring to a boil again, then reduce the heat, cover, and simmer until the rice is tender, about 30 minutes.

2 Meanwhile, in a large saucepan, melt the butter over medium heat. Sauté the carrots and celery in the butter until slightly browned, about 4 minutes. Add the broth and thyme, and season with pepper. Simmer over medium heat until the vegetables begin going soft, 20 minutes.

3 Drain the rice and add it to the broth along with the chicken, mixing gently with a wooden spoon. Heat through, 5 minutes. Serve hot.

TURKEY
BURGERS

SERVES 4

I love turkey burgers. Unfortunately many turkey burgers on restaurant menus involve bread crumbs and such; so did my mama's turkey burger. And our Rebekkah's turkey burger. My recipe is all righteousness—so many good flavors and no naughty fillers.

1 teaspoon salt

1 tablespoon dried oregano

1 teaspoon ground cinnamon

½ teaspoon cayenne pepper

½ teaspoon paprika

½ tablespoon garlic powder

1¼ pounds ground turkey

3 tablespoons olive oil

1 Using a wooden spoon, stir together the salt, oregano, cinnamon, cayenne, paprika, and garlic powder in a large bowl. Add the turkey and mix well. When the spices are evenly distributed into the turkey, stir in 2 tablespoons of the olive oil.

2 Heat the remaining 1 tablespoon olive oil in a frying pan, preferably cast-iron, over medium-high heat. Form the turkey mixture into 4 burgers. Cook in the pan until done all the way through, about 6 minutes on each side.

JOAN'S NIÇOISE
WITH OKRA LADYFINGERS

SERVES 4

The downtown campus of Tennessee State University is now named the Avon N. Williams campus, in honor of Nana's husband, my grandfather. Though today the school graduates often become doctors and lawyers and nurses and teachers, TSU's origins as an agricultural institute devoted to creating scientific farmers is revealed by the acres it still has under cultivation. In fact, the campus is now part of the cutting-edge phenomenon of urban black gardeners. And the "Ag School" at TSU is enjoying a renaissance as sustainability, food justice, and food security become frontline issues across the United States. The summer of 2013, TSU gardens were enjoying a bumper crop of okra and some of the gardeners were pickling it. That's what inspired this salad.

Okra is an acquired taste—unless it's pickled. Cooked most ways, okra can be peculiarly or wonderfully slimy, depending on whether you have acquired a taste for it. Pickled okra is crisp and earthy, with an astringent bite. While we know precious few people who put up their own cucumber pickles these days, for some reason a lot of our friends like to pickle their own okra.

It is thought that *okra* is an Igbo word and one of the few African words to remain intact in the English language. In some parts of the English-speaking world, the vegetable is referred to as "ladyfingers." We named our version to honor a woman who worked her fingers to the bone in support of the movement and didn't, like her husband, get a building named after her. Joan would have preferred a dish, anyhow, and this dish is honest and just plain good with pickle-bite, like the lady herself.

Acknowledging that most of us don't make time to pickle our own okra, and because it's what Joan would have used, this recipe uses store-bought—but home-pickled is best.

2 tablespoons Dijon mustard

3 tablespoons red wine vinegar

1 tablespoon olive oil

Salt and pepper

1 new potato, as large as you can find

1 To make the salad dressing, whisk the mustard, vinegar, and olive oil together in a small bowl, and season with salt and pepper.

2 Put the potato in a saucepan with enough lightly salted water to cover, bring to a boil, and cook until tender when pierced with a knife, about 12 minutes.

16 asparagus stalks

1 head romaine lettuce

2 hard-boiled eggs (see page 99)

2 large tomatoes, sliced

2 (2-ounce) tins anchovies

2 (5-ounce) cans tuna, drained

4 pickled okra

3 Meanwhile, bring a deep skillet of salted water to a boil and add the asparagus stalks. Cook until crisp, about 5 minutes. Cool under cold running water. Drain well.

4 Tear the romaine into bite-size pieces, and divide them among four plates. Slice the eggs crossways, so you have disks with the yolk in the middle. Arrange the egg slices along one edge of each plate. Lay slices from half of 1 tomato on top of the romaine on each plate. Place 4 asparagus stalks across the top of the salad, then add about 5 anchovies, a quarter of the tuna, and 1 pickled okra, using your own instincts to help you make the plate good looking! Drizzle with the dressing, and serve.

COUNTEE AND YOLANDE'S
POACHED SALMON
WITH LEEKS

SERVES 4

This dish is simple but it has pretensions. I first made poached salmon and leeks in Oxford, England, when I was in a period of life my students would have described as "bougie," or bourgeois. I named it for Harlem Renaissance poet Countee Cullen and Harlem Renaissance princess Yolande Du Bois. Shortly after their wedding, the preeminent social event of the Harlem Renaissance, they moved to Europe, where Yolande, under strict instructions from her father, W. E. B. Du Bois, attempted to do all she could to support Countee's writing. I have imagined some of the "all" was to cook delicious meals that reminded him not at all of the country they had left—the one to which she returned when the marriage fell apart. Two years after Arna watched eighteen bridesmaids walk down the aisle ahead of Yolande, she was in Baltimore teaching school and Countee was still in Paris writing. I named this dish as a warning to myself. I first started cooking it to help a boyfriend through his final Oxford exams.

1 tablespoon butter

1 tablespoon olive oil

4 cups chopped leeks, white and light green parts (about 5 large leeks)

5 tablespoons heavy cream

1/3 cup dry white wine

Salt and pepper

1 pound boneless, skinless salmon fillet, cut into 4 pieces

3/4 cup chopped fresh parsley

1 In a saucepan, heat the butter and oil over low heat. Add the leeks and cook until they are very soft, about 5 minutes. Add the heavy cream, cover, and turn off the heat but leave the pot on the still-warm burner.

2 To poach the salmon, pour the wine and 2/3 cup of water into a nonreactive skillet that can go into the oven. Season with salt and pepper. The liquid should taste a bit like the sea. Add the salmon and 1/2 cup of the parsley, and simmer over medium heat until the salmon is opaque at the center, 8 to 10 minutes.

3 Turn the heat under your leeks back onto low, to reheat them. Remove the salmon from the cooking liquid and transfer it to plates. Pour the cream and leeks over the cooked salmon. Sprinkle the remaining parsley on top.

SHRIMP
STEW

SERVES 6

In many a Louisiana family in the early days of the twentieth century, this dish would be on the stove at least once a week. In the twenty-first century we've come to think of it as special-occasion or party food, if we think of it at all. Usually the shrimp stews are forgotten in favor of the shrimp Creoles.

Grandma cooked shrimp Creole. She would make a roux just about the color of my arm. Making that nut-colored roux is the secret to getting the tomato sauce to cling to the shrimp. Without a roux you've got a stew. Committed to renovating the soul food kitchen, Mama gave up the true Creoles in favor of the fewer carbs and fewer calories in the otherwise identical and incredibly flavorful shrimp stew. This is a favorite dish of mine.

2 cups chopped onion

2 garlic cloves

2 tablespoons olive oil

3 large green bell peppers, seeded and chopped

5 green onions (white and green parts), chopped

2 cups chopped celery

4 cups diced tomatoes (fresh or canned)

1 tablespoon Worcestershire sauce

2 pounds peeled and deveined medium shrimp

4 bay leaves

1 teaspoon cayenne pepper

1 teaspoon salt

1 bunch fresh parsley, chopped (reserve some for garnish)

Cooked rice, for serving

1 In a large pot, cook the onion and garlic in the olive oil over medium heat until the onions soften, about 5 minutes. Add the bell peppers, green onions, and celery, and cook for another 5 minutes. Add the tomatoes, Worcestershire sauce, shrimp, bay leaves, cayenne, salt, and parsley, and simmer over medium-low heat for 1 hour.

2 Ladle the stew over hot rice in individual bowls. Garnish generously with parsley.

SALMON CROQUETTES
WITH DILL SAUCE

SERVES 8

These are straight old-school. Canned salmon formed into a patty and fried was dinner and supper and sometimes even breakfast in many a hardworking black household in the middle of the twentieth century. Salmon had the advantage over many other proteins of being relatively nonperishable, inexpensive, and pretty in pink to boot.

Back in the day, salmon croquettes usually meant rich bindings and fillers. Everything from eggs, flour, cracker crumbs, and béchamel sauce has been used to hold them together. And back in the day they were typically fried in an inch of bacon grease. In my house, the binder is egg only, and the patties are pan-seared in a little olive oil. Sometimes I serve them over a salad, sometimes I plate them with vegetables, and sometimes I put them in a bun for a salmon alternative to beef or turkey burgers.

The French name always reminds me of my Louisiana roots: a Bontemps eating a *croquette*, right? This dish smells so good when it's cooking that my dog won't give me a second of peace.

1½ cups plain yogurt or fat-free sour cream

¼ cup Dijon mustard

6 sprigs fresh dill, chopped

2 (14.75-ounce) cans salmon packed in water (look for a sustainable brand)

4 celery stalks, finely chopped

1 large white onion, finely chopped

4 large eggs, beaten

½ tablespoon salt

1 tablespoon pepper

2 tablespoons olive oil

1 To make the dill sauce, whisk together the yogurt, mustard, and dill in a small bowl. Set aside.

2 Drain the salmon, and then remove and discard the bones and skin. Mix the salmon, celery, onion, eggs, salt, and pepper in a good-size bowl. Form the mixture into 8 patties. Slick a medium skillet with the olive oil and heat it over medium-high heat. Cook the patties until browned on both sides, about 5 minutes per side.

3 Put a dollop of the dill sauce on top of each patty, and serve.

NOTE If you want a slightly more old-school, firmer croquette, simply add ¾ cup plain dry bread crumbs to the mix.

SHRIMP
SALAD

SERVES 10

Next time you want to bring a big old bowl of salad to a potluck, I hope you think of this dish. It's delicious, it's beautiful, it fills you up, and it's good for you. It's one of my favorite things to make in summertime. You can fix this dinner without turning on a stove.

2 pounds deveined cooked shrimp

4 large green bell peppers, seeded and sliced into strips

1 head romaine lettuce, chopped

1 red onion, sliced and separated into rings

1½ cups crumbled aged feta cheese

¼ cup olive oil

½ cup red wine vinegar

½ teaspoon pepper

Toss all the ingredients together in a large salad bowl, and serve! It's that easy!

NOTE If you take a moment to look for certified Wild American Shrimp, Marine Stewardship Council, or Best Aquaculture Practices stickers or symbols, you are much more likely to be eating shrimp that has been harvested with an attention to the state of the planet. Eating shrimp can be done with tenderness to the environment or can be part of an environmental disaster. Unless you're at the shore or know your fisherman, just buy frozen. Most of what's sold "fresh" has previously been frozen.

GEORGE'S
RED SNAPPER

SERVES 4

Minnie served fish on Fridays. Always. Even after the Pope said it wasn't necessary. Bobby Dunlap, who grew up working in Dear and Paw Paw's cleaners and was in and out of their house, becoming a kind of fifth son and a best friend to middle son George, remembers picking up the fish from the neighborhood fishmonger many a Friday early afternoon: "I didn't even have to say what I wanted. I just had to say I was there for Mrs. Randall's order and they would know exactly how many pieces of perch and how they should be fixed."

When George got older he preferred red snapper, an Alabama fish. Descended from both slaves and slave owners, George was deeply conflicted about his Alabama roots. He avoided the state quite literally like the plague, going there only on rare occasion and under duress until 1981, the year his youngest daughter, my mama, graduated from college. At the graduation he said he was forgiving America. Afterward he traveled to Selma. He reported being astounded to see black and white children swimming together in a Holiday Inn pool. "I expected, one day, to see angels eating manna. I didn't expect to see black kids in swimming pools in Alabama." The luxury of an integrated clear-water swimming pool, not a murky-water river, was a "kingdom come" moment for George. He celebrated by eating red snapper.

2 skinless red snapper fillets
(about 1 pound total)

2 tablespoons olive oil

1 lemon, cut in quarters

A few sprigs fresh oregano

A few sprigs fresh parsley

½ lime

1 Preheat the oven to 400°F.

2 Divide both fillets in half. Put each piece in the middle of its own square of aluminum foil. Drizzle the snapper with the olive oil, and squeeze one quarter of the lemon over each fillet. Cover each fillet with oregano and parsley sprigs. Fold the aluminum foil in toward the middle so that each fillet is fully wrapped. Fold and pinch the edges to seal completely. Put the packets on a baking sheet. Bake until the fish is cooked through, about 10 minutes.

3 Carefully open the foil packets (there may be a lot of steam), transfer the fillets to plates, and squeeze the lime over them. Serve immediately.

RED AND BLACK BEAN
BURGERS

SERVES 6

This is one of my favorite dishes, especially in the springtime, when I want the spirit of a burger and want to empty my winter pantry! One of the things I also like about these burgers is that they don't taste as if they're trying to be something they're not; they're just doing their own delicious thing, though they are nice with all the classic burger fixings.

1 medium red onion, chopped

1 garlic clove, chopped

4 tablespoons olive oil

1 (16-ounce) can red kidney beans, rinsed and drained

1 (16-ounce) can black beans, rinsed and drained

1 cup rolled oats

½ tablespoon dried oregano

1 teaspoon chili powder

1 teaspoon paprika

Salt and pepper

1 In a small skillet, cook the onion and garlic in 2 tablespoons of the olive oil over medium heat until softened, about 5 minutes.

2 Meanwhile, mix together the red and black beans, rolled oats, oregano, chili powder, and paprika in a large mixing bowl, using a heavy wooden spoon. Season with salt and pepper. First you want to make sure the spices get evenly distributed throughout. Then you want to start smashing enough of the beans so that the bean mixture will hold together and form a patty. Incorporate the onion mixture into the bean mixture. Form into 6 (¾-inch-thick) patties.

3 To cook the burgers, slick the skillet with the remaining 2 tablespoons olive oil, and heat over medium-high heat. Cook the burgers until the oats begin to crisp, about 6 minutes per side. Serve hot.

SWEET POTATO, KALE, AND BLACK-EYED PEA
SOUP

SERVES 8 TO 10

This is a perfect soup for everyday eating throughout the fall and winter, but it's also delicious enough to be on the stove for a giant New Year's Day party—or to be served as company supper—particularly when garnished with fresh thyme. We've used it for our Southern Festival of Books party and to entertain any number of foodies. Another plus? It totes well. Put some in a mason jar and take it to a friend who's feeling low. She can remove the lid, nuke it in the jar, and serve herself an easy dinner made by loving hands at home. If you do serve it on New Year's Day, chock-full of black-eyed peas and greens, it is sure to bring good luck and prosperity.

1 tablespoon olive oil

1 large onion, diced

1 large carrot, sliced

1 celery stalk, sliced

3 garlic cloves, chopped

5 sprigs fresh thyme

1 tablespoon dried thyme

¼ teaspoon crushed red pepper flakes, or more to taste

1 quart Sweet Potato Broth (page 104)

1 (14.5-ounce) can diced tomatoes, including juice

8 cups kale leaves, collards, or mustard greens, torn

2 (15-ounce) cans black-eyed peas, rinsed and drained

Salt

1 Heat the olive oil in stockpot over medium heat. Add the onion, carrot, and celery and cook, stirring, until the vegetables just begin to get soft, about 5 minutes. Add the garlic, fresh and dried thyme, and crushed red pepper. Keep stirring. Pour in the sweet potato broth and tomatoes with their juice. Keep stirring. Raise the heat to high, bring to a boil, and add the kale. Cover, reduce the heat, and simmer for 45 minutes.

2 Add the black-eyed peas and continue to simmer, covered, until the flavors meld and the greens are completely tender, about 15 minutes more. Season to taste with salt, and add more red pepper flakes if desired.

RED BEAN AND BROWN RICE
CREOLE SALAD

SERVES 8

This is a great tote-along veggie main course dish. It is super quick and easy, can be served cold or at room temperature, and is delicious.

½ cup chopped celery

¼ cup chopped onion

¼ cup chopped green bell pepper

2 tablespoons olive oil

¼ cup red wine vinegar

3 drops Tabasco sauce

Salt and pepper

1 (16-ounce) can red kidney beans, rinsed and drained

4 cups cooked brown rice

1 Put the celery, onion, bell pepper, olive oil, vinegar, and Tabasco in a mason jar. Screw the lid on tight and shake vigorously. Add salt and pepper to taste. Shake again.

2 In a large bowl, fold the red beans into the brown rice, using a spatula. Douse liberally with the Creole dressing and chill for at least 1 hour and up to overnight. Serve cold.

OAKWOOD
BEAN LOAF

SERVES 6 TO 8

This recipe reminds me of the days Grandma spent at Oakwood, a historically black Seventh-day Adventist college in Huntsville, Alabama, where she lived in a falling-down antebellum mansion while Arna wrote *Black Thunder: Gabriel's Revolt: Virginia, 1800.* Grandpa taught there in the early 1930s and so Grandma did a whole lot of vegetarian cooking (Adventists believe that "flesh food" should be avoided). This is my updated version of a traditional black Adventist bean loaf.

Mama says bean loaf reminds her of the Black Muslim bean pies of her Washington, D.C., childhood. Those are a bit sweet. This one is spicy.

3 tablespoons vegetable oil, plus more for the pan

1 cup quinoa, rinsed and drained

Salt

1 (16-ounce) can red kidney beans, rinsed and drained

1 small onion, chopped

8 ounces grated cheddar cheese (2 cups)

1 tablespoon crushed red pepper flakes

3 drops hot sauce

2 large eggs, beaten

¼ cup chopped green onion (white and green parts)

1 Preheat the oven to 350°F. Oil a 9 x 5-inch loaf pan.

2 In a small saucepan, combine the quinoa with 2 cups of water and season with salt to taste. Bring to a boil over medium heat. Lower the heat, cover, and simmer until the water is absorbed and the quinoa is tender, 15 to 20 minutes. Uncover and let cool for 5 minutes; then fluff with a fork.

3 Whirl the beans in a food processor until chopped.

4 Cook the onion in the vegetable oil in a skillet over medium heat until soft, 5 minutes. Transfer to a large bowl and set aside to cool.

5 Mix the beans, cheese, red pepper flakes, and hot sauce into the onion. Season with salt. Now stir in the eggs and quinoa. Transfer to the loaf pan and smooth the top. Bake until a knife stuck in the center comes out clean, about 1 hour.

6 Let the loaf cool in the pan for 5 to 10 minutes; then unmold it. To serve, slice the loaf and top the slices with the chopped green onion.

POET'S
POT PIE

This is a vegetarian shepherd's pie with sweet potato mash. This pie is rich, down-home, colorful, and cheap. It's everything a thriving kitchen should be.

Salt

3 large sweet potatoes, quartered

¼ cup plus 2 tablespoons olive oil

2 yellow onions, chopped

1 cup chopped carrots

2½ cups fresh or thawed frozen lima beans

1½ cups fresh or thawed frozen green peas

1 cup fresh or thawed frozen corn

1 cup heavy cream

1½ tablespoons dried oregano

½ teaspoon ground cloves

½ teaspoon ground nutmeg

Pepper

1 Fill a medium pot with water and season it with salt. Toss in the sweet potatoes, making sure the water covers them, and bring to a boil. Reduce the heat and simmer until the sweet potatoes are tender when pierced with a knife, about 20 minutes.

2 Meanwhile, preheat the oven to 400°F.

3 While the sweet potatoes are cooking, slick the bottom of a large skillet with the 2 tablespoons olive oil. Cook the onions over medium heat until they soften, 5 minutes. Add the carrots and lima beans, cover, and cook for another 5 minutes. Add the peas, corn, cream, oregano, cloves, and nutmeg; season with salt and pepper. Turn the heat up to medium-high and cook until the cream begins to reduce and thicken, 2 minutes or so. Remove from the heat. Pour the mixture into a 9-inch pie dish.

4 Drain the sweet potatoes and then mash them with a large spoon, or with a masher if you've got one. As you mash them, slowly pour in the remaining ¼ cup olive oil. Season with salt and pepper to taste. Spoon the sweet potatoes on top of the lima bean mixture, making sure to spread them evenly on top so that the entire dish is covered. Bake until heated through and browned, 40 minutes. Serve hot.

SIDES
&
SALADS

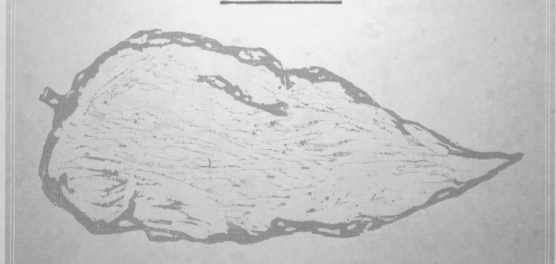

A MESS OF
GREENS

SERVES 10

These are our culinary legacy, the green that never stops growing and is a part of our inheritance. Picking greens. Washing greens. Cutting greens. Simmering greens. In the 1970s and '80s there were lots of recipes that focused on getting a smoky flavor into the greens without cooking them with salty meats. By the time I started cooking greens, I only distantly remembered the pots of greens Nana and Grandma cooked that included smoked turkey legs and even ham hocks. I was far more familiar with Caribbean-style greens—hot, spicy, and stewed with other vegetables, the heat replacing the smoke. That's what happens here.

2 large bunches collards, kale, turnip greens, or mustard greens

1 yellow onion, diced

3 garlic cloves, minced

3 jalapeños, diced

¼ cup hot sauce

1 tablespoon apple cider vinegar

1 I like to wash my greens seven times, but I realize that isn't essential. It is, however, essential that you wash them in enough changes of water to get them completely clean. After you wash them, tear them up and throw them in a large pot. Add 1½ quarts of water, the onion, garlic, jalapeños, hot sauce, and vinegar, cover the pot, and bring to a boil. Reduce the heat, and allow the greens to stew on low heat until very soft, 2 hours.

 Serve the greens hot with plenty of the pot liquor.

SIMPLE
SPINACH

SERVES 2

Spinach can be a false friend. Spinach dip. Creamed spinach. Back in the day, on her way to weighing way more than two hundred and twenty pounds, Mama made a "Plain Thanksgiving Spinach" dish that took three or four days of cooking and involved sautéing fresh spinach in butter, then refrigerating it and sautéing it in *an additional quarter pound of butter a day every day for four days* until the spinach had absorbed *more than an entire pound of butter*. I'm not going to lie and say it didn't taste good because it was the best green butter I ever tasted. I wanted to spread it on bread. Even as a child I knew that was no vegetable.

We've retired that dish. Good as it was, there's no place for it even once a year. It's something that almost stole Mama from me. My spinach is a true and old friend. And it tastes plenty good enough for the Thanksgiving table.

Spinach is the first vegetable I ever learned to cook all by myself. I was so young, I said things like "easy-peasy." Actually, I'm dragging that phrase out and dusting it off. This recipe is easy-peasy. This is the simplest cooked side dish in my repertoire.

6 cups tightly packed fresh
  spinach

½ lemon

Salt and pepper

Rinse the spinach in a colander. Do not shake off the excess water. Put the spinach in a large pan, sprinkle with a couple flicks of water, and squeeze the lemon juice over it. Cover the spinach and cook over low heat for about 8 minutes, until it is dark green and wilted. Season with salt and pepper to taste, and serve.

BOILED
ARTICHOKES

SERVES 4

"Mommy, artichoke, please." That was my first full sentence, or so I've been told. We were living in Martinique at the time—my dad was in the Foreign Service. When I did finally speak up, it was a great relief to my mother. I had barely said "baa" for milk, didn't say "Mama," and in general had been uncharacteristically mute for a Randall or a Williams. Thinking back on it now, it's no surprise that it was a food request that loosened my tongue.

Boiled artichokes are a specialty at our house, as a starter, a favorite salad, or sometimes dinner itself. They are dramatic, easy, and tasty. The only drawback is that artichokes can be expensive. We say about artichokes what Art Buchwald was rumored to have said about caviar: When you can get it, splurge. And unlike caviar, an artichoke is a splurge most of us can manage to afford, at least sometimes.

4 teaspoons red wine vinegar

8 whole cloves

Salt

4 artichokes

1 lemon, halved

4 tablespoons olive oil

Pepper

1 Fill a stockpot two-thirds full with cold water. Add the vinegar and cloves, and season generously with salt. Bring to a boil over high heat.

2 Meanwhile, trim the artichokes: Cut the tip off one artichoke. Cut the thick stem off the base. Using vegetable scissors or any clean large scissors, cut off the sharp tips of the leaves. As you cut, rub the cut edges of your artichoke with the lemon halves. Repeat with the remaining artichokes.

3 Submerge the artichokes in the boiling water. Return the water to a boil, cover the pot, and reduce the heat. Simmer until the artichokes are tender when the base is pierced with a knife, about 45 minutes.

4 Drain the artichokes. (You can serve them hot or cold; chill if desired.) Drizzle 1 tablespoon of olive oil on each of 4 saucers. Sprinkle with salt and pepper, and top each pool with an artichoke. To eat, peel off the leaves and scrape off the flesh from the bottom of each leaf with your teeth. Cut out the fuzzy choke with a knife and eat the heart with a fork.

ARTICHOKE FOREST We often serve this for Christmas. The method is the same as on the opposite page except we do not trim the leaves and do not cut the pointed tip off the artichokes. With tips and tops on, the artichokes resemble mini Christmas trees. Twelve or more on a platter resemble a forest. (If small children will be eating from your forest, you will want to cut off the tips of their artichoke leaves, however, as these are sharp.) You can use your imagination to create ornaments and tree toppers. In the past I've used a star anise for the topper and pieces of red bell pepper as ornaments.

BROCCOLI
WITH PEANUTS AND RAISINS

SERVES 8

My mama raised me in restaurants but begged me to cook at home when I started out in the world. Mama said, "Do as I say, not as I do." I'm trying. But I, too, love a restaurant.

From the moment it opened in a sculptor's studio in East Nashville, City House was our kitchen across town. Tandy Wilson's cooking is stripped down and sound. Tandy cooks a lot of pork. His flavors are bold, bright, and clean. Nothing fussy, little sweet. He serves a lot of his vegetables raw and the most delicious broccoli we have ever tasted. If you've got a hard case who claims not to like broccoli, try this as a bridge back to the basics of veg.

1 cup unsalted peanuts

6 tablespoons olive oil

1 cup raisins

Salt

4 broccoli stalks with large crowns

Pepper

1 Start by putting the peanuts in a small cast-iron pan over medium heat. Add enough olive oil (about 3 tablespoons) to cover them halfway. Gently fry the peanuts until golden brown, then remove from the heat, and stir in the raisins. Salt the peanuts and raisins to taste, then keep stirring for another 30 seconds or so. Remove from the heat.

2 Preheat the oven to 450°F.

3 As the oven is heating up, cut the stalks off of the broccoli crowns and then break the crowns down into small florets. Chop the stalks into bite-size pieces. Mix the broccoli and the remaining 3 tablespoons of olive oil in a large bowl, adding salt and pepper to taste, and then spread it out on a baking sheet. Roast in the oven until the broccoli is well browned but still has a little crunch, about 10 minutes.

4 Remove the broccoli from the oven, put it in a serving dish of your choice, and top with the peanuts and raisins.

ROASTED ASPARAGUS
WITH LEMON ZEST

SERVES 4

When serving asparagus hot, this is our preferred way of cooking it. There's a smoky richness to the roasted asparagus flavor that we adore.

Mama also prefers roasting asparagus because it tastes different from the asparagus she grew up eating, which was boiled standing up in the pan, tied together with a twist of aluminum foil. That was the asparagus she ate in the country house her mother shared with a significant other in Virginia, not far from the mansions of Middleburg. They grew asparagus on that hobby farm, along with corn and strawberries. They also grew sorrow too sharp and bitter to share.

Mama's told me precious little about her time in the country. What I know is this: It was on those Virginia acres that she learned the true meaning of the phrase "back-breaking labor," and it was on those acres, isolated and injured, that she truly began to imagine herself in the lives of her ancestors who had been enslaved. Like going back to the kitchen, going back to the farm is not a simple act for black women. That my mother could see the beauty in the asparagus grown tall and spindly despite having first seen it on acres where generations of black women had been owned and she herself was persecuted is a triumph of will and perception.

That it's my favorite late-night snack if I've got folks coming over is a triumph of the old informing the new, and finding a way to thrive together.

1 bunch asparagus
2 tablespoons olive oil
Grated zest of 1 lemon
Salt and pepper

1 Preheat the oven to 375°F.

2 Cut the tough ends off of the asparagus (about ¾ inch above any visible white on the spear). Line a baking pan with aluminum foil, and spread the asparagus out in the pan. Drizzle the olive oil over the asparagus, scatter the lemon zest on top, and then sprinkle with salt and pepper. Get in there with your hands to rub the mixture into the stalks. Roast until tender but not droopy, 25 minutes.

ROASTED
GREEN ONIONS

SERVES 4

Green onions are one of God's gifts that don't need much help to taste delicious. Fresh, they have a brash and powerful flavor. Roasted, the flavor relaxes into something bold, a little sweet, a little sharp.

According to cooking lore, our ancestresses carried a taste of their African homes with them to the New World—sesame seeds hidden in their hair. Thomas Jefferson wrote that the sesame seed "was brought to S. Carolina from Africa by the negroes. . . . They bake it in their bread, boil it with greens, enrich their broth, &c."

The sesame seeds that garnish our onions give this dish a straight taste of Africa.

3 bunches (about 15) green
   onions (white and green
   parts), peeled and trimmed

1 tablespoon olive oil

Pinch of salt

3 tablespoons sesame seeds

1 Preheat the oven to 400°F.

2 Toss the green onions with the olive oil and salt on a baking sheet. Roast until the onions have browned but aren't completely limp, about 12 minutes. Sprinkle with the sesame seeds before serving.

ANY DAY
SNAP BEANS

SERVES 4

I have great memories of sitting in Nana's kitchen snapping green beans. Whether you call them string beans, snap beans, pole beans, or half-runner beans, these are a universal favorite to cook in black Southern kitchens and to grow in black home gardens. Green beans on a pole are the one vegetable Dear allowed to be planted in her backyard garden. Not with the roses, of course, but on a pole off to the side of the garage.

Mama can be a food snob. She hates frozen vegetables. I don't—and that's a big part of why I'm skinnier than Mama. Frozen vegetables in the freezer can mean the difference between eating home and not eating home. And frozen vegetables allow us to capture summer all winter long. As the brilliant Maya Angelou noted in her cookbook *Hallelujah! The Welcome Table,* a black woman can't afford to turn her nose up at anything but evil. Frozen vegetables are not evil. If you live in a food desert, frozen vegetables can be your salvation. I know they were mine when I moved to the Delta!

1 pound fresh or frozen green beans

1 bunch fresh chives

2 tablespoons olive oil

Salt and pepper

NOTE When poking around at the farmer's market, don't get too excited when you come across strikingly beautiful purple-podded snap beans. Though they are delicious, you should know that the purple beans turn green when cooked.

1 For fresh green beans: Snap both ends off of each bean. Wash the beans in a colander that's the right size to suspend in a pot by the handles. Fill a large pot halfway with water and bring to a boil. Set the colander of beans over the boiling water, cover with a lid, and steam until crisp-tender, about 10 minutes. While the beans are steaming, chop the chives.

2 For frozen green beans: Cook according to the package instructions. While the beans are cooking, chop the chives.

3 However you cook them, when the beans are done, toss them with the olive oil, then sprinkle with the chives. Serve hot. (If you're going to serve the green beans cold, dunk them in a bowl of ice water to set the green color.) Season with salt and pepper before serving.

A COLD HOT
RADISH SALAD

SERVES 6

My mother loves radishes. Which is perhaps not surprising. Radishes are fiery and sweet, just like Mama. Plus they're beautiful to look at. In our house, "bite the radish" is shorthand for "face the pain and get on with it."

Mama was finishing writing a movie script when her daddy, whom I called Granddaddykins, died. In the days after he was buried, as the script deadline loomed, she spent more hours frozen in her bed than writing. Fortunately the phone rang and it was the man she called Godfather, Bob Glynn. She asked him hopelessly, "What am I going to do?" He said, "Bite the radish and move on." Mama burst out laughing. It was the first time she had laughed since Granddaddykins's passing. I asked why she was laughing and she told me what Bob Glynn had said. It made no sense to me. It was only later that I encountered *Gone with the Wind*. The one scene I love is where Scarlett digs up the radish in the yard, vomits, then makes a promise to herself that neither she nor her family will ever be hungry again. (I don't think my Mama likes any part of *GWTW*.)

With this salad we're making a new promise: that our family will never be poorly fed again. This salad packs a punch of flavor that helps knock out hunger.

8 watermelon radishes
  (see note)

1 bunch fresh chives

¼ cup olive oil

Salt and pepper

Slice the radishes as thin as possible, and arrange them on a serving plate. Chop the chives into ½-inch pieces, and scatter them on top. Drizzle with the olive oil, and dust the salad with salt and pepper.

NOTE Watermelon radishes are especially pretty, but if you can't find them, any pink radish will do.

FIERY
GREEN BEANS

SERVES 4

Fire!! was a literary journal that put out only one issue but was very influential. We created this dish to celebrate Wallace Thurman, Zora Neale Hurston, Aaron Douglas, Richard Bruce Nugent, Gwendolyn Bennett, Countee Cullen, and Langston Hughes, and the incendiary spirit behind the publication. According to Hughes, the point was to "burn up a lot of the old, dead conventional Negro-white ideas of the past." Ironically—and horrifically—the offices of *Fire!!* burned to the ground shortly after the first publication.

In the spirit of *Fire!!* we challenge the notion of what a soul food green bean recipe can be. This recipe is a luminous example of the new old-school. Mama and I went to eat at a hip, more than a little bougie burger joint. We saw green bean salad on the menu and thought, let's see what they're doing in that kitchen. The beans they sent out were so good, we asked to meet whoever had dreamed them up. A young black man in a chef's jacket came out to the table. He'd scribbled the recipe from the top of his head onto a piece of scrap paper. "Glad y'all liked it," he said. We asked him if we could share his new soul truth with the rest of the world in our cookbook. Nashville is known for its hot chicken. We would far prefer Nashville to be known for its hot green beans.

2 tablespoons fresh lemon juice

1 green onion (white and green parts), thinly sliced

1 tablespoon chopped fresh parsley

1 teaspoon chopped fresh cilantro

1 teaspoon crushed red pepper flakes

1 pound fresh green beans, ends snapped

2 tablespoons olive oil

Salt and pepper

1 Preheat the oven to 375°F.

2 In a bowl or measuring cup, spike your lemon juice with the green onion, parsley, cilantro, and red pepper flakes.

3 Put the green beans on a foil-lined baking sheet. Drizzle with the olive oil. Roast for 10 minutes. Switch the oven to "broil" and broil until browned in spots and just tender, about 4 minutes.

4 Remove the baking sheet from the oven, and splash the spiked lemon juice over the green beans. Season to taste with salt and pepper. Serve hot, or refrigerate and serve cold. These just get better as they sit.

SWEET POTATO
SKEWERS

SERVES 6

My stepfather grew up spending summers with his grandparents on the campus of Tuskegee University, where George Washington Carver was long a professor. The Carver Museum was his favorite hangout. Carver invented numerous items made from sweet potatoes, from flour and mock coconut to dry paste. He also created or popularized dozens of recipes involving the sweet potato. This is a sweet potato recipe George Washington Carver *didn't* come up with! Onions and sweet potatoes complement each other perfectly, sort of like Mama and Bopy.

1 large yellow onion

2 large sweet potatoes

½ tablespoon paprika

½ tablespoon olive oil

Salt and pepper (optional)

1 Preheat the oven to 400°F. Soak six 10-inch wooden skewers in water for 20 minutes.

2 Quarter the onion and break up the quarters so that you have two or three layers of onion per piece. Quarter the sweet potatoes, then chop them so each sweet potato yields about 12 roughly shaped chunks. Thread the sweet potato and onion chunks onto the skewers, alternating the vegetables, until the skewers are full. Put the skewers on a baking sheet, sprinkle with the paprika, and then drizzle with the olive oil. Bake until the sweet potato chunks are tender when pierced with a knife, about 20 minutes.

3 Our taste calls for no salt or pepper added to this one, but your taste may be different. Season with salt and pepper if desired.

DEFORD'S SPICY ROASTED
SWEET POTATOES
WITH POMEGRANATE

SERVES 10

Some say there are two kinds of jazz playing: hot and sweet. I say the best has both. DeFord Bailey was the best. A black man and a star on the Grand Ole Opry, he is now too often forgotten. His instrument was the harmonica and he did amazing things with it. He was also a friend of the family who once recorded a jingle for my grandpa Avon when he was first running for state senate. I named this dish in honor of DeFord.

Just like Mr. Bailey's music, this dish has got a whole lot of hot and sweet in it. I served it to producer Ken Burns when he was first coming to Nashville to make a documentary on the history of country music. I know they are not going to overlook my man DeFord. In the George Washington Carver Food Park in Nashville there is a rose garden dedicated to DeFord Bailey. He's buried in Greenwood Cemetery not far from Grandma and Grandpa Bontemps.

Watch out for this recipe—don't serve this with spicy chicken (see page 122) unless you want your mouth *on fire* for the rest of the night. I learned that one the hard way.

3 large sweet potatoes, cut into
   ½-inch chunks

Salt and pepper

2 fresh hot red chile peppers

1 garlic clove

⅓ cup red wine vinegar

1 tablespoon honey

3 tablespoons olive oil

1 medium red onion, chopped

2 cups pomegranate seeds
   or unsweetened dried
   cranberries

1 Preheat the oven to 400°F.

2 Put the sweet potatoes on a baking sheet, season with salt and pepper, and roast until tender when pierced with a knife, about 20 minutes.

3 While the sweet potatoes are roasting, make the dressing: Seed and chop the chile peppers. Transfer them to a food processor and add the garlic, vinegar, and honey. Whirl until finely chopped. Slowly pour in the olive oil with the motor running, and whirl until the dressing is smooth.

4 Toss the sweet potato chunks with the onion, pomegranate seeds, and dressing. Serve hot or cold.

LINKS
SALAD

SERVES 10

Mama, Nana, and Grandma were all Links. Actually, Mama is still a Link. The Links, Incorporated, is sometimes called the black Junior League. Mama invented this salad—which is green and white, Links colors, but doesn't involve lettuce—for her Links club meeting when she was first starting to think about healthy eating.

I fixed this dish at one of my earliest Sunday dinners in Oxford, Mississippi. It's the first recipe I served that people asked me how to make for themselves. Links Salad is just that good, and that simple to make.

I strongly suspect this will be on the menu at my first club meeting—if I get to be a fourth-generation Link. If I get to be one soon, I've been told I will be the first fourth-generation Link in the country.

1½ pounds fresh green beans, ends snapped

1 cup fresh or frozen green peas

¼ cup olive oil

Salt

4 cucumbers, peeled and sliced

16 fresh basil leaves

2 lemons, halved

Pepper

1 Steam the green beans (see page 154) and set them aside to cool.

2 Using the same method, steam the peas until just cooked, about 2 minutes. Set the peas aside to cool.

3 Pour the olive oil into a large bowl. Whisk in 1 teaspoon salt. Toss the beans and peas with the salted olive oil.

4 Stir the cucumbers and the basil into the green beans, and toss to combine. Squeeze the juice of the lemons over the vegetables, season with pepper, and toss again. Serve at room temperature or chilled.

WARM ONION AND ROSEMARY
SALAD

SERVES 8

The dining table in the house where I grew up seats eighteen people. We moved into the house when I was about twelve. Soon after, we started holding casual supper parties, inviting the families of my friends from Sunday school. These would usually be cold suppers: half a roast salmon, two kinds of vegetables, and a caramel cake. Because nothing had to be heated up, it was a very easy meal to get onto the table. Over the years we moved to more and more cold dishes. I started to miss hot food, particularly in the wintertime. This salad was invented for a winter baby shower. We made lots of roasted baby vegetables in honor of the occasion, but this cozy, simple dish was my favorite.

3 large yellow onions
10 sprigs fresh rosemary
3 tablespoons olive oil
Salt

1 Preheat the oven to 350°F.

2 Quarter the onions and spread them out on a foil-lined baking sheet. Pull the needles off of the rosemary sprigs, and scatter the needles over the onions. Drizzle with the olive oil and season with salt. Roast until the onions are translucent, golden brown, and fragrant, about 25 minutes. Serve warm.

SAVORY AVOCADO SALAD
WITH CORN, PEPPERS, AND CILANTRO

SERVES 10

In Louisiana, where my great-grandfather Arna Bontemps was born, avocados are sometimes called "alligator pears." There's something a little dangerous, and a little exciting, about that name. I love avocados. Grandma said Arna loved them, too; that he associated avocados with California and opportunity, and with Mexico and inspiration. I seek ways to include them in my meals; they are the healthiest kind of buttery.

Arna had a close friend, writer and photographer Carl Van Vechten, who was known to close a letter or two with the words "avocadoes and Mexican jewelry to you." Van Vechten was also a dear friend of Langston Hughes, who was Grandpa Bontemps's best friend. This salad honors one of Grandpa Bontemps's many collaborations with Langston: the children's book *The Pasteboard Bandit,* set in Mexico. Avocado, corn, and peppers make very good friends, much like Arna, Lang, and Carl.

4 cups corn kernels (see note)

3 large red bell peppers, diced

4 large avocados, diced

1 bunch fresh cilantro, chopped (about 1 cup)

Juice of 2 limes

2 tablespoons olive oil

Pepper

1 Toss the corn, bell peppers, and avocados in a salad bowl with ⅔ cup of the cilantro.

2 To make the salad dressing, puree the remaining cilantro with the lime juice in a blender or food processor, slowly adding the olive oil. Dress the salad and add pepper to taste. An hour in the refrigerator improves this dish.

NOTE If corn is in season, use fresh kernels cut from the cob; you'll need about 4 large ears. The rest of the year, simply steam frozen kernels until tender and then let cool.

RESURRECTION SALAD
WITH GRILLED PLUMS

SERVES 8

In some parts of the South and Appalachia, killed lettuce, where a hot dressing wilts the greens, is a familiar dish. We love these kinds of salads, but instead of thinking about how we're killing the lettuce, we're thinking about how we're eating fresh greens to revive ourselves, and to resurrect our sense of Southern food as something that takes care of us.

I met my mama's mother, the Lutheran Lady, only once that I recall. This is because when I was too young to remember, the Lady insisted on her right to tell me I was too dark and too fat, so Mama put her in what turned out to be a very long time-out. When the Lutheran Lady was sick and dying, we went to see her. She greeted me with a barbed compliment: "You're tall, you're trim, you do math; unlike other people in this room, you've got it all." That was her first sally. When it got bad enough, I whispered to the witch that if she said another mean word to my mama, we were leaving. When we left, I told Mama she was my she-ro. I also told her I never needed to see that grandmother again.

Lutheran Lady was born in Ironton, Ohio, a furnace town on the West Virginia border, during a killing flood. It was hell on earth. Men worked in the foundries till they died, and their women quietly shivered, making do on starvation wages. There's an Appalachian salad called "kilt salad" that's made by drowning lettuce in bacon grease. Designed to fuel manual laborers, it's now killing the descendants of those laborers.

I've reimagined that salad as a prayer for my maternal grandmother. I've taken the grace-filled fruits of my healthy foremothers—the plums from the garden of my great-grandmother Alberta and the apricots from my great-aunt Mary Frances—and used that abundance to replace the flavorful pig fat.

We buried the Lutheran Lady at sunrise. We walked to the grave on my stepfather's family farm in darkness. Mama's friend sang a song that Mama had written for her birth mother. In the song she spoke directly to Eve, who was sitting with Jesus. Mama asked Eve to speak to Jesus on Lutheran Lady's behalf. She imagined Eve would understand and forgive a woman who had made many mistakes. When I heard the song I knew one day I would create something that would show the peace I would make with the woman. This salad is that thing.

½ cup sliced green onions (white and green parts)

½ cup olive oil

¼ cup red wine vinegar

¼ teaspoon salt

½ teaspoon pepper

4 plums, pitted and chopped

4 apricots, pitted and chopped (or additional plums)

½ teaspoon crushed red pepper flakes

2 heads romaine lettuce, torn into pieces

1 In a small saucepan, heat the green onions, olive oil, vinegar, salt, and pepper over medium heat. Bring to a simmer, then add the chopped fruit and red pepper flakes. Bring to a boil. Cover, and reduce the heat so the dressing simmers until the fruit is soft, about 10 minutes.

2 Divide the lettuce among eight plates and pour the hot dressing over the greens.

NEW-SCHOOL
"FRUIT" SALAD

SERVES 8

Fruit salad is a soul food staple. Whether we're talking about delectable-enough-for-the-Christmas-table ambrosia, or old-school fruit cocktail eaten straight from the can, mixed fruits in various forms and fashions were served in Dear's, Grandma's, Nana's, and Mama's kitchens.

But let's just admit right now that commercial fruit cocktail is an abomination that should never be served to anybody's child. The way the fruit is processed, there's almost no fiber, few vitamins, too much sugar, and too many calories. It needs to be stricken from school cafeteria menus, from recipes, and from pantry shelves. Instead, make this new-school fruit salad, which tastes great, looks beautiful, packs nutrients, and rights old wrongs.

What other old wrong might that be? Stigmatizing eating watermelon. We know black families who refuse to this day to let their children eat watermelon in public because they don't want to reinforce stereotypes. But guess what? Watermelon is a fat-free taste treat that everyone should enjoy. So we chop what was traditionally sliced and introduce new fruits to the mix. As an added bonus, this salad is also something of a botany lesson. Many people forget that avocados are fruits. Same with tomatoes. This recipe is a tasty reminder.

3 tablespoons olive oil

Juice of 1 lemon

Pinch of salt

2 pinches of pepper

¼ medium watermelon, preferably seedless

1 cup cherry tomatoes, quartered

2 avocados, diced

¾ cup crumbled feta cheese

1 Whisk the olive oil, lemon juice, salt, and pepper together in a small bowl.

2 Remove the rind from the watermelon and chop the flesh into ½-inch cubes. Combine with the tomatoes and avocados in a serving bowl, and gently toss. Add the feta cheese and the dressing, and toss again.

CHOPPED
SPINACH AND
TURKEY SALAD

SERVES 4

I was determined to find a way to like raw spinach. Chopping the greens within an inch of their lives and adding a little mint did it for me. The trick to a great chopped salad is to get the various bits into fairly uniform-size pieces. Chopped salads have a neat and constructed appearance, in contrast to full-leaf tossed salads that have a wild and whimsical look. You can enhance this appearance when serving this salad by molding it in a teacup or a square cake pan before turning it out onto a plate or platter.

1 (7.5-ounce) jar marinated artichoke hearts packed in oil

2 cups chopped roasted or smoked turkey

5 cups tightly packed chopped fresh spinach

1 cup loosely packed chopped fresh mint

2 tablespoons Dijon mustard

¼ cup balsamic vinegar

Salt and pepper

1 Drain the artichoke hearts, setting aside 2 tablespoons of the oil for the salad dressing. Chop the hearts. Toss the artichoke hearts, turkey, spinach, and mint in a large salad bowl.

2 To make the salad dressing, whisk together the mustard, reserved oil, and the balsamic vinegar. Dress the salad, season to taste with salt and pepper, and serve.

HERBED
CORN ON THE COB

SERVES 4

We seldom eat corn without remembering the role it played in the slave trade. Corn was cultivated in Africa by slave traders to increase profits by fattening up captured Africans for market. On the other hand, many Native Americans consider corn a sacred food and we consider Native Americans a sacred people. Corn should effectively remind us that all food choices are political choices—and that few foods are only good or only bad.

Cooking corn for the table is as simple as pulling off the husks, stripping off the fine silks, plopping the corn into boiling water, waiting for the water to return to a boil, then removing the corn from the pot. This is easy unless you have a crowd coming. Then it is far easier to cook corn in the oven, wrapped in foil. You can stack forty or more ears of corn on two oven shelves. If you're cooking forty ears of corn, you're probably having a party. To add to the festivities, we like to use olive oil to paste herbs onto our ears of corn before roasting them. This is pure deliciousness.

2 tablespoons olive oil

1 tablespoon dried oregano

Pinch of salt

Pinch of cayenne pepper

4 ears of corn, husks and silks removed

1 Preheat the oven to 350°F.

2 Mix the olive oil, oregano, salt, and cayenne in a small bowl. Rub each ear of corn with the herb mixture and then wrap them individually in aluminum foil. Roast until tender, 20 minutes. Unwrap and serve.

NOTE Many different herbs can be laid inside the corn packet: basil, parsley, and tarragon are among our favorites.

OLD-SCHOOL
SALAD PLATE REVISITED

SERVES 8

Salad in the South doesn't always mean lettuce. In fact, when you see "salad plate" on a menu, if you're like me, you imagine something with meat and mayonnaise. I grew up on chicken salad in Nashville. Mama grew up on tuna salad in Detroit, where everyone called jars of Miracle Whip "salad dressing"—that's how familiar the chopped protein, mayonnaise, and celery concoctions were. On the soul food table, "salad" can also mean fruit suspended in Jell-O and molded into a Bundt pan. We don't play that. Here are two healthier options: one with a mustardy Greek yogurt dressing and the other with an herbed vinaigrette. They make a nice luncheon plate when served together.

FOR THE CHICKEN SALAD

3 cups cubed steamed chicken breast (see page 120), cold

4 hard-boiled eggs (see page 99), chopped, cold

5 celery stalks, chopped

3 tablespoons Dijon mustard

½ tablespoon celery seeds

½ cup Greek yogurt

Salt and pepper

FOR THE TUNA SALAD

3 (5-ounce) cans tuna packed in water, drained

½ cup olive oil

¼ cup chopped fresh tarragon

2 tablespoons fresh lemon juice

Salt and pepper

4 avocados, halved and pitted

TO MAKE THE CHICKEN SALAD: Combine the chicken, eggs, and celery in a large mixing bowl. In a small bowl, whisk the mustard and celery seeds into the yogurt. Fold the yogurt mixture into the chicken mixture. Season with salt and pepper. Scoop onto plates.

TO MAKE THE TUNA SALAD: Combine the tuna, olive oil, tarragon, and lemon juice in a medium mixing bowl. Season to taste with salt and pepper. Scoop the tuna salad into the avocado halves and place on the plates, snuggled up to the chicken salad.

DESSERTS

MERINGUES

JUGGED PEAR

CHOCOLATE COMMUNION

HONEY PEANUT BRITTLE

FLAN

SINLESS SWEET POTATO PIE

SPIKED WATERMELON

MERINGUES

MAKES 2 DOZEN 2-INCH MERINGUES

For me meringues are a near-perfect dessert. They are sweet and crunchy, and embody a bit of cooking magic. I grew up eating these little clouds of joy. Among Nana's cookbooks, one of the real rarities is *The Frances Parkinson Keyes Cookbook*. Keyes was a popular early twentieth-century novelist who settled in New Orleans and wrote extensively about culinary Louisiana. Just above a Maple Mousse that Keyes claims as "F.P.K.'s Own Invention," she provides a meringue recipe that is simplicity itself. In fact, it's so simple that someone who doesn't know how to make meringues probably would end up with a gooey mess following the instructions. Keyes assumes we know things that have been lost as culinary literacy has declined.

My mother shelves the Keyes cookbook beside *Cross Creek Cookery* by Marjorie Kinnan Rawlings, the Florida novelist who wrote *The Yearling* and was friends of a sort with Zora Neale Hurston. Mama believes the folksy Rawlings would drive the fancy Keyes crazy. I think they're both a mess. Kinnan's book includes a recipe for "Utterly Deadly Southern Pecan Pie." In her recipe for "My Reasonable Pecan Pie" she writes, "I have nibbled at the Utterly Deadly Southern Pecan Pie and I have served it to those in whose welfare I took no interest."

In contrast, here's a recipe with full instructions that I would be happy to serve to those I love. I try to do as my mother has come to do: limit myself to eating the sweets I make myself, sweets I would truly be unable to cook myself, or those made by someone who loves me and are given as a gift. It doesn't mean I eat no sugar; it does mean I eat less.

3 large egg whites, at room temperature

1 cup sugar

1 teaspoon pure vanilla extract

1 Preheat the oven to 250°F. Line a baking sheet or two with parchment paper.

2 Beat the egg whites with an electric mixer until they begin to form peaks. Beat in ½ cup of the sugar, teaspoon by teaspoon, until the meringue thickens and becomes shiny. Switch to a rubber spatula and fold in the rest of the sugar. Fold in the vanilla. Drop the meringues by the heaping table-spoon onto the parchment paper. Bake until crisp, 30 minutes.

3 The meringues will crisp up further as they cool at room temperature. When cool, use a sharp-edged spatula to remove them from the parchment paper. Store in an airtight container if you are not serving immediately.

VARIATIONS Once you can whip up a meringue with ease, many variations are possible. My favorite: add a tablespoon of instant coffee with the last of the sugar. Or you can add a tiny pinch of flaky sea salt, such as Maldon, to the top of the meringues before baking if you want to get really fancy.

If you are preparing the meringues for a wedding, birthday, or other important event, you can take them from everyday to festive by making them with vanilla sugar instead of regular sugar: The day before making the meringues, put the sugar you will be using in a jar with a tight-fitting lid and add a vanilla bean—split it lengthwise, scrape out the seeds, and add the seeds and bean to the sugar. Remove the vanilla bean (save it for another use) before using the sugar in the recipe. If you do this, you won't need the teaspoon of vanilla, unless you want, and I often do, a very strong vanilla flavor.

JUGGED PEAR

SERVES 6

There is perhaps no dish I associate with Mama more than this one, her version of Dear's dress-box apples. Deep purple, jewel-like, and magical, her pears poached in red wine and spices were the centerpiece of our large Christmas breakfasts or Christmas supper open houses. We would spend days locating a hundred or more small pears, then a night peeling and a night poaching.

These need no adornment or additions to make a perfect dessert. They can also elevate a plain lettuce salad at a luncheon. Served with Greek yogurt, these pears make an excellent simple but fancy breakfast.

When choosing your red wine for poaching, pick an inky red that's fruit forward, typically a Zinfandel or a Syrah. Don't poach the pears in a wine you wouldn't drink, but it doesn't have to be an expensive bottle.

6 ripe but firm pears

1 (750-ml) bottle red wine

½ cup sugar

Zest from 1 lemon, removed with a vegetable peeler

16 whole cloves

½ tablespoon ground cinnamon

½ tablespoon ground nutmeg

1 Peel the pears, and cut off the bottoms so they can sit up when you plate them. Pour the wine into a large saucepan and set it over medium heat. Add the sugar and stir until it dissolves; continue to stir occasionally until the wine comes to a boil. Turn down the heat so that the wine simmers. Add the lemon zest, cloves, cinnamon, and nutmeg, and finally the pears. Make sure the pears are submerged in the wine. Then reduce the heat to low, cover the pan, and simmer until the pears are very dark and tender when pierced with a knife, about 45 minutes.

2 Carefully remove the pears from the liquid and let both the pears and the liquid cool. Once cool, the pears can be stored overnight in the cooking liquid; they will take on the most beautiful color and profound flavor.

3 Serve the pears in a pool of their poaching liquid.

CHOCOLATE
COMMUNION

SERVES 50

Dark chocolate and a thimble-full of bourbon—dessert couldn't be simpler or more elegant. We invented this for a party when we were doing all the cooking and expecting more than a hundred guests. On that occasion we spread brown butcher paper down the center of our library table and served several varieties of chocolate. Communion cups can be purchased in large quantity for a small price, typically a hundred cups for less than five dollars. If you can't find disposable communion cups, small Dixie cups could work.

The National Institute of Health is currently researching the health benefits of dark chocolate. Some theorize that it could possibly have a positive impact in helping folks recover from, or not develop, a variety of maladies from high blood pressure and diabetes to certain cancers. Dr. Luc Djoussé of Harvard Medical School has found an overall drop in blood pressure among people who eat dark chocolate, with more benefit to those who already have high blood pressure. Milk chocolate and white chocolate are not associated with health benefits. Neither is bourbon. But we like it, especially with chocolate.

1 (750-ml) bottle of bourbon

24 ounces dark chocolate, broken into shards

Give each guest a communion cup full of bourbon, then pass around a tray of chocolate.

NOTE We recommend Belle Meade bourbon and Olive and Sinclair chocolate when you serve Chocolate Communion. The two horses on the bourbon label remind us of Bob Green, the African American man who, both before and after Emancipation, bred the ancestors of a good many of the horses that have won the Kentucky Derby on a plantation called Belle Meade. If you can't get Olive and Sinclair chocolate, Walmart carries the Green & Black's brand of dark chocolate.

HONEY
PEANUT BRITTLE

MAKES 12 PIECES

Tammy Horn is a professor at Berea College who wrote *Bees in America: How the Honey Bee Shaped a Nation*. She notes that many enslaved African Americans came from beekeeping countries and brought their honey-hunting skills to America. From looking at recipes and songs, she concludes that some Africans used honey before coming to America and incorporated it into plantation menus. Native American groups bartered beeswax and honey with enslaved people as well as French traders and English, German, and Dutch settlers.

This candy deliciously celebrates those all but forgotten intertwinings in early American society. It also celebrates George Washington Carver, who advocated for everything peanut—as well as sweet potato. And, for us most important, it celebrates B.B. Bright, the fairy-tale princess I invented in the doctor's office when I was about three. B.B. is a brown beekeeper.

If you're going to eat candy, we think you should make it. Having to make my own certainly cuts down on the amount of candy I eat.

1 tablespoon unsalted butter, plus more for the pan

4 cups dry-roasted peanuts

1 cup sugar

1 cup honey

½ teaspoon fresh lemon juice

1 tablespoon baking soda

Pinch of salt

1 Butter a baking sheet.

2 In a deep pot, bring the nuts, sugar, honey, and lemon juice to a simmer over high heat, mixing constantly to make sure not to burn the sugar. Boil the sugar mixture until it reaches 300°F on a candy thermometer. (If you don't have a candy thermometer, another way to test the temperature is to drop a bit of the mixture into a glass of ice water. If it hardens, you're all set!) Once the sugar begins to darken, carefully stir in the baking soda, butter, and salt. The sugar will fluff up from the baking soda, so be careful. Pour the brittle mixture onto the prepared baking sheet and allow it to cool completely before breaking it into pieces.

3 Put the brittle in a sealed container or plastic bag, and store it somewhere cool and dry—if you've got any left once you've tasted it!

FLAN

This just may be the perfect dessert. It is made with simple ingredients, can be made well ahead, is pretty, and involves a bit of drama in its presentation. And it's a world traveler. In French-speaking communities, this dish is often known as *crème caramel,* and it appears in many old Creole cookbooks. In the Philippines it's known as *leche* flan. My first nanny, Leedy Ellacer, fondly known as Yaye, loved this dish. I love it, too.

Flans don't always love you back—they can be just a bit finicky. You've got to cook a flan slowly and evenly, or instead of a silky interior you'll have something grainy at worst and full of little bubbles if it's just slightly off. And making caramel is not the easiest kitchen task, but once you've taught yourself it's like riding a bike—you won't forget and you'll love it when you get the chance.

1½ cups sugar

6 large eggs

⅛ teaspoon salt

3 cups whole milk, warmed

1 tablespoon pure vanilla extract

1 teaspoon ground nutmeg

1 Preheat the oven to 325°F. Have ready six 6-ounce ramekins.

2 To make the caramel, stir 1 cup of the sugar with ½ cup of water in a small saucepan. Bring the liquid to a boil over high heat, and continue to boil, swirling the pan and checking the sugar until it becomes amber colored. Remove from the heat and carefully pour the hot caramel into the ramekins. Tilt and swirl the ramekins to make sure the caramel spreads over the bottom of each dish and slightly up the sides. Let sit until the caramel hardens, a minute or two.

3 To make the custard, whisk together the eggs, remaining ½ cup sugar, and the salt, then mix in the milk, vanilla, and nutmeg. Pour this mixture on top of the hardened caramel in the ramekins.

4 You will have to make a water bath to bake the flan. To do that, use a small roasting pan or large baking dish, and fill it halfway with hot water. Then put the ramekins in the pan; the water should come three-quarters of the way up the sides. Carefully transfer the pan to the oven and bake until the custards are just set, about 50 minutes. To cool, remove

the pan from the oven, then remove the ramekins from the hot water. They can cool on any heat-resistant surface or on a rack if you have one. Once they have cooled, refrigerate the flans until fully chilled, at least 5 hours.

5 To unmold the flans, set the ramekins in an inch of hot water for 30 seconds. Dry the bottoms, then run a flexible spatula around the inside edge of each ramekin. Invert a plate over each ramekin and then flip the plate and ramekin together so the plate is right side up. Give the bottom of the ramekin a firm thwack with a wooden spoon before lifting off the ramekin.

SINLESS SWEET POTATO
PIE

SERVES 8

Though Dear mainly cooked only her exquisite dishes—the spectacularly colored candied apples, the dazzling ice cubes, and the dainty crustless shaped sandwiches—she did on occasion make sweet potato pie . . . without a crust.

This pie dials back the butter and sugar from Dear's version and ups the warming spices. With respect we add pecans. Dear's hometown of Selma, Alabama, is famous for them.

1 tablespoon unsalted butter, plus more for the dish

3 sweet potatoes, cooked (see note)

⅓ cup honey

½ tablespoon fresh lemon juice

1 teaspoon pure vanilla extract

1 teaspoon ground cinnamon

1 teaspoon ground nutmeg

¼ teaspoon ground cloves

⅓ cup packed dark brown sugar

2 large eggs, beaten

1 cup ground toasted pecans

1 Preheat the oven to 400°F. Butter a 9-inch deep-dish pie pan.

2 Peel and quarter the sweet potatoes and put them in a very large bowl. Using an electric mixer, whip the sweet potatoes until smooth. If you need to, stop to remove the strings from the beaters before continuing to whip. Add the honey, lemon juice, butter, vanilla, cinnamon, nutmeg, and cloves.

3 Melt the brown sugar in a small saucepan on very low heat, stirring and watching constantly. When the sugar is melted, whirl it into your sweet potato mixture. Whirl in the eggs. Finally, fold in the pecans. Transfer the sweet potato mixture to the prepared pan. Bake until a knife stuck in the middle comes out clean, about 45 minutes.

NOTE To cook a naked sweet potato, all you have to do is wrap it in foil and bake it in a 375°F oven for 1 hour. Or microwave it, unwrapped, at medium-high power for about 10 minutes. It's done when you can stick a fork in it and the fork can go all the way through. After that, slice it lengthways, pull it open, and eat. The sensualists in our family prefer their sweet potatoes scantily clad. For those hedonists I rub each sweet potato with 1 teaspoon olive oil, then sprinkle it with a pinch each of salt and pepper before baking.

SPIKED
WATERMELON

SERVES 16

As far as fruits go, watermelon is a bit more expensive in terms of carbs and calories than an apricot, but if you're comparing it to a piece of cake it's a bargain, even when spiked. Needless to say, this one's not for the kids! Watermelon is a festive fruit that screams "summer." And somehow for me, it screams "defiance," a refusal to be stereotyped. This watermelon is literally intoxicating. We deal in the real. This dish acknowledges an overlooked fact: some moonshiners were black!

1 large seedless watermelon (7 to 10 pounds)

1 cup moonshine, tequila, or spirit of your choice

1 Take an empty 12-ounce water bottle, turn it upside down, and hold the mouth to the watermelon as a guide. Use a sharp knife to cut around the mouth of the bottle. Remove a good piece of watermelon. Set it aside to use as a plug. Insert the knife into the hole and stick it at various angles to make sure that the liquor will be able to diffuse throughout the fruit. Pour the spirit into the water bottle, then flip the bottle quickly and insert the mouth into the watermelon. You'll want to do this as fast as you can so you don't spill. It will take a while for the spirit to seep all the way into the watermelon, so carefully move the watermelon, with the bottle, to the refrigerator. If it's going particularly slowly, you can periodically take the water bottle out and poke more holes into the flesh of the watermelon to help it spread through faster.

2 Serve chilled and sliced into individual wedges.

WATERMELON SHOTS Use a melon baller to make watermelon spheres or balls. Put the balls in a zip-top plastic bag and add the spirit. Refrigerate for at least an hour. These can be served in a glass bowl with toothpicks.

CROWNS

MOLDED MULATTO RICE

CAULIFLOWER CROWN

EGGPLANT TOWER WITH MASHED WHITE BEANS

SALMON MOUSSE

CREPE STACK

MOLDED
MULATTO RICE

SERVES 12

Crowns are what folks in our family call the tall, and often round, dishes that we present to our most cherished guests to signify their preciousness. Molded Mulatto Rice is a favorite crown of mine.

Plain "Mulatto rice" is the name of the dish Pheoby brings Janie in the opening of Zora Neale Hurston's American masterpiece *Their Eyes Were Watching God*. Unfortunately no one knows for sure what that dish is. As much as rice is white, we can assume that mulatto rice is in some way colored. It could be saffron rice, bright yellow, but as saffron was not readily available in rural Florida in the early days of the twentieth century, this seems unlikely. Brown rice is also a possibility. It could be rice cooked with bits of offal. Sometimes this dish is called "dirty rice" because of the flecks of brown, but it seems rather unlikely that Hurston would name a dish "mulatto" that was typically called "dirty"—or would she? So this dish is pure invention. I wanted something that was a warm welcome home that included a bit of brown in the white. I decided to add mushrooms because they can be foraged and they seem in keeping with the spirit of *Their Eyes Were Watching God,* which is so much about the beauty and danger of living off the land. Mushrooms are the blowfish of soul food. Dangerous beauties. I also decided to make the dish with brown rice. Typically we don't stir rice as it is cooking. By stirring this dish you give it the stickiness that allows you to mold it and turn it into a crown.

1 medium yellow onion, chopped

2 tablespoons olive oil, plus more for the bowl

2 cups chopped mushrooms

Salt and pepper

3 cups brown rice

2 cups chopped tomatoes (canned or fresh)

In a large pot, cook the onion in the olive oil over medium heat until it softens, 5 minutes. Add the mushrooms, season with salt and pepper, and continue to cook for 2 minutes. Add the rice and cook, stirring constantly, for another minute. Add 6 cups of water and bring to a boil. Cover the pot, lower the heat, and simmer for 20 minutes. Uncover, stir in the tomatoes, and cook, now stirring constantly, until the rice is tender and has absorbed all of the water, about 10 minutes. Season with salt and pepper if needed.

2 Slick a mold of your choice—a bowl will work
perfectly—with a little olive oil, transfer the rice to the
mold, pack it down with the back of a spoon, and allow the
dish to settle for at least 20 minutes.

3 Run a flexible spatula around the inside edge of the mold
to loosen the rice. Flip the mold over onto a platter,
thwack it two or three times on the bottom with a wooden
spoon, and then carefully lift off the mold. Serve hot.

CAULIFLOWER
CROWN

SERVES 6

I first ate a bite of whole roasted cauliflower at Domenica in New Orleans. A year later
I returned to the city with my mother for Essence Fest. We stayed in the Quarter, on the
concierge floor at the Omni Royal Orleans, and had the time of our lives with sisters from all
over the country. Everyone told us not to stay in the Quarter during Essence—too crowded,
too loud—but everyone was wrong! If we hadn't been in the Quarter it would have been
difficult to walk to Domenica, and we wouldn't have met the original Mouse (think Walter
Mosley) riding the tables at the Carousel Bar. Sharing Alon Shaya's cauliflower, Mama and I
almost simultaneously remarked that it was akin to eating monkey bread—your piece came
from the whole and the whole looked like a crown. But it was so much healthier and—forgive
us, Godmommy Lea—even more delicious. Our version of this dish doesn't involve a whipped
cheese, wine, or sugar like the original, but we still think it's delicious.

⅓ cup red wine vinegar

1 teaspoon dried rosemary

1 bay leaf

1 large head cauliflower, any
  green leaves removed

3 tablespoons olive oil

Salt and pepper

1 Preheat the oven to 450°F.

2 In a large pot, combine the vinegar, rosemary, and bay
leaf with enough water to cover the cauliflower, and
bring to a boil over high heat. Add the cauliflower and reduce
the heat. Simmer the cauliflower until you can easily stick a
knife through it, about 30 minutes.

3 Drain the cauliflower and transfer it to a baking dish. In
a small bowl, whisk the olive oil with salt and pepper to
taste, and pour this evenly over the cauliflower. Bake, standing upright on its base, until well browned, about 30 minutes.

EGGPLANT TOWER
WITH MASHED WHITE BEANS

SERVES 4

I first ate a dish something like this at a coffee shop called Fido near our house in Nashville. It's in an old pet shop. This is a simple, quick, and yet dramatic dish that's perfect for every day or for special occasions. I decided to put it in the cookbook when I was Skyping with my best friend, Read, who was living in Africa. He said to me, "Hey, I've got some garlic, some eggplant, some tomatoes, and some beans. What do I do with them besides chop them all up and throw them in a pot?" I love it when food makes the world smaller. These ingredients are found across the globe, and so close to my roots.

1 (15.5-ounce) can white beans

3 garlic cloves

4 tablespoons olive oil

Salt and pepper

2 large eggplants

4 large tomatoes

1 Heat the beans and their liquid in a small saucepan. Once they begin to bubble a bit, transfer them, together with the garlic and 2 tablespoons of the olive oil, to a food processor. Whirl until smooth. Add salt and pepper to taste. Scrape the bean mixture back into the saucepan and return it to very low heat while you prepare the eggplant and tomatoes.

2 Cut the ends off of each eggplant and discard. Slice the eggplants and tomatoes into ½-inch-thick disks. Set the tomato slices aside. Working in batches and using the remaining 2 tablespoons olive oil, cook the eggplant in a skillet over medium-high heat until browned, about 5 minutes per side.

3 To serve, make a tower for each person by layering 3 eggplant slices and 3 tomato slices with the white bean puree.

SALMON
MOUSSE

This is the kind of dish Grandma loved. It is a perfect fancy party food that can be made on the cheap and in advance. If Nana was making it, she would have added Louisiana brand hot sauce, taken out the dill, and thrown in a bit of cayenne pepper to turn this elegant mousse into something suitable for a bar. And she might have served it on cucumber slices. On this occasion, I prefer Grandma's way.

2 (14.75-ounce) cans salmon

1 envelope unflavored gelatin

½ cup boiling water

½ cup mayonnaise

1 tablespoon fresh lemon juice

2 tablespoons finely chopped sweet Vidalia onion

2 tablespoons chopped fresh dill, plus more for serving

½ teaspoon paprika

1½ cups cottage cheese

Salt and pepper

Vegetable oil for the mold

1 Start by draining, then carefully picking over, the salmon (you want to remove and discard any skin, bones, and brown bits). Chop the salmon coarsely; you should have at least 3 cups.

2 Put ¼ cup of cold water into a large bowl. Sprinkle the gelatin over the top. Allow it to soften for 2 to 3 minutes. Then add the boiling water and stir until the gelatin dissolves. Set aside to cool for 5 minutes.

3 Stir the mayonnaise, lemon juice, onion, dill, and paprika into the cooled gelatin mixture. Stir in the chopped salmon.

4 In a blender or food processer, whirl the cottage cheese until it has a silky-smooth texture. Fold the cottage cheese into the salmon mixture. Add salt and pepper to taste.

5 Oil a fish mold, bowl, or other mold that has a capacity of 1 to 1½ quarts. Pack the salmon mixture into the mold and refrigerate for at least 3 hours or overnight.

6 To unmold, sit the mold in a larger pan of hot water for a minute or two. Dry the mold, then run a flexible spatula around the inside. Invert over the plate on which it will be served, then give the mold a firm *thunk* with a wooden spoon before lifting off the mold. Garnish with dill, and serve.

CREPE STACK

Growing up, I had a wide variety of stunningly beautiful and dramatic birthday cakes that all had two things in common: they didn't begin in a box and they had many, many layers. My mother baked from-scratch strawberry cakes, five layers of home-baked cake interspersed with five layers of homemade strawberry filling. Once assembled, the whole luscious stack would be frosted with two pounds of sweet butter into which cups and cups of white sugar and the very best Madagascar vanilla had been hand-whipped—because that's how my family does it.

Or *did* it, I should say. Because when Mama finally realized that a cake like that might mean fewer birthdays, she decided to tweak our tradition.

My birthday cakes are still tall and homemade, only now the layers are thin crepes and the fillings are less sugary. And I don't always wait for a birthday to whip up a crepe stack. Filled with fresh strawberries and minted cream or homemade applesauce, and garnished with herbs in place of frosting, the cake is six inches tall and looks gorgeous with or without candles. It honors the cakes that Alberta, Joan, and Alice made, but it's quicker than the old cakes, cheaper than the old cakes, and healthier than the old cakes. You can make it in an hour using tablespoons—not cups—of sugar and flour.

6 large eggs

¼ cup all-purpose flour

2 tablespoons whole milk

⅛ teaspoon salt

8 tablespoons (1 stick) unsalted butter, plus more for the pan, at room temperature

½ cup granulated sugar

½ cup fresh mint leaves, plus more for serving

1 cup plain yogurt (I prefer Greek)

4 cups thinly sliced fresh strawberries

Confectioners' sugar (optional)

1 To make the crepes, whisk together the eggs, flour, milk, 2 tablespoons of water, the salt, and the butter in a large mixing bowl. Slick a medium skillet (8 or 9 inches across) with a little butter. Heat the skillet over medium-high heat until the butter just sizzles but does not brown. Scoop enough of the crepe mixture into the skillet to thinly cover the bottom, and immediately swirl the skillet to spread out the batter. Cook until set and lightly browned, 2 to 3 minutes. Flip and cook the second side for a minute or two until golden brown. Set aside on a plate. Continue making crepes until all of the batter is used up—you should be able to make about 6 large crepes. Stack them on top of each other as you go.

(RECIPE CONTINUES)

APPLESAUCE CREPE STACK For a winter version of the crepe stack, we omit the strawberries and make a quick homemade apple-sauce to use for the filling. Peel, core, and slice 4 large apples. Put them in a medium saucepan and add just enough water to cover them. Dust with cinnamon, and simmer, covered, until the apples turn to a mush you can whip with your whisk. Let cool before using. Garnish the crepe stack with sprigs of fresh rosemary if desired.

2 Heat the granulated sugar and 1 cup of water in a small saucepan over medium heat, stirring until the sugar dissolves and the mixture comes to a simmer. Add the mint leaves and simmer for another 2 minutes. Remove from the heat and set aside to cool.

3 To make the filling, use a blender to puree the cooled mint syrup with the yogurt.

4 Put the crepe stack together by placing the first crepe on a serving platter, adding a layer of strawberries, and then drizzling the yogurt sauce over them. Add another crepe, and then another layer of strawberries, and so on until you run out! Sprinkle with confectioners' sugar if you like, and garnish with mint leaves. Pour the remaining yogurt sauce into a small serving pitcher so people can add more if they like. Cut the stack into slices, and serve.

FOR A CROWD

BILL'S WHOLE SMOKED TURKEY

ROASTED LEG OF LAMB

MOORISH PIZZA

HERB-ROASTED SALMON FILLET

BREAKFAST CASSEROLE

GRANDMA'S CHIA PUDDING

BILL'S WHOLE
SMOKED TURKEY

SERVES 10 TO 20

Bill is my step-grandmother's significant other. A retired banker, he is also a great cook. Back in the 1950s his family owned and ran a restaurant in North Nashville. For the holidays he often brines and smokes a turkey for us. This is his recipe. Aside from being tasty, it celebrates the fact that black men have long been associated with barbecue culture in the American South—as well as with hunting, fishing, and liquor distilling. In Nashville, black men are also associated with the tradition of the fish fry, in which fried fish is served alongside spaghetti with red sauce, often at a church or community fundraiser or political rally. A smoked turkey is healthier.

1 gallon hot water

1 pound kosher salt

1 pound honey

2 quarts Sweet Potato Broth (page 104) or low-sodium vegetable broth

1 (7-pound) bag of ice

1 (15- to 20-pound) turkey

Vegetable oil

Low-sodium vegetable broth, for basting

1 Combine the hot water and the salt in an immaculately clean 54-quart cooler. Stir until the salt dissolves. Add the honey and stir until it too dissolves. Stir in the sweet potato broth. Finally, add the ice. This is your brine.

2 Remove and discard the giblets, neck, and any other parts that have been put in the turkey's cavity. Rinse the turkey thoroughly inside and out with cold water. Put the turkey in the brine, making sure it is fully submerged. Put the top on the cooler and put the cooler in a cold place; a large refrigerator is ideal. If you live in a cold climate, a back porch or basement may work. However you manage it, the turkey and the turkey brine *must* stay below 40°F while the turkey brines for 12 hours.

3 The next day, heat a grill or smoker to 400°F. Soak 1 cup of hickory chips in cold water for 30 minutes while the grill heats.

4 Remove the turkey from the brine and pat it dry thoroughly. Rub the turkey all over with vegetable oil. Put the turkey in a large heavy-duty disposable aluminum pan. Tent it loosely with foil.

5 Drain the hickory chips and add them to the hot coals. Put the turkey pan (uncovered) on the grates of the grill. Cover and smoke, adding hot coals as needed every half hour or so to maintain the temperature, until a meat thermometer placed in a thigh reads 180°F. As it is cooking, do as Bill does and baste the turkey with vegetable broth.

6 When the turkey is done, remove it from the fire and let it rest for at least 20 minutes before carving and serving. We particularly enjoy this turkey served cold after chilling overnight in the refrigerator.

ROASTED
LEG OF LAMB

SERVES 10

This dish is a forgotten soul food Easter classic, and a tradition I'd like to revive. Learning to roast lamb right, I pored through the many recipes Nana had marked in her one thousand cookbooks. I'm proud to feed my family with this dish because it offers a taste of the non-bar food of Nana.

1 (5- to 7-pound) bone-in leg of lamb

6 garlic cloves, minced

2 tablespoons Dijon mustard

2 tablespoons fresh or dried rosemary

3 tablespoons balsamic vinegar

2 tablespoons olive oil

1 tablespoon salt

1 teaspoon pepper

1 Put the leg of lamb in a roasting pan. In a small bowl, mix together the garlic, mustard, rosemary, vinegar, olive oil, salt, and pepper. Rub the mixture thoroughly into the lamb, cover with plastic wrap, and refrigerate overnight.

2 The next day, preheat the oven to 375°F.

3 Roast the lamb until the internal temperature is between 145° and 150°F, about 1½ hours. After you take the meat out of the oven, let it rest for about 20 minutes before you slice and serve.

MOORISH
PIZZA

Necessity is the mother of invention. We came up with this recipe when we had to entertain a crowd of more than a hundred on the cheap but with a bit of elegance in the middle of summer. It was too hot to order pizza—and pizza just didn't have the requisite glam. We loved the idea of some kind of meze meal, but the idea of hundreds of little bowls or hundreds of people dipping in and out of the same large bowls failed to appeal. When the pizza wish and the Mediterranean meze platter idea collided, this Moorish pizza was born. We've cut the proportions down, assuming you want to feed a smaller army.

1½ cups hummus (see page 92)

8 (12-inch) pitas

1 cup baba ghanoush (see page 97)

2 tablespoons chopped fresh parsley

½ teaspoon ground coriander

2 tablespoons olive oil

Spread the hummus on top of the pitas, leaving about ½ inch bare around the edge. Spread the baba ghanoush on top of the hummus in a slightly smaller round. Sprinkle the parsley on top, followed by the coriander. Then lightly drizzle olive oil over the whole pizza. Cut into wedges to serve.

HERB-ROASTED
SALMON FILLET

SERVES 6 TO 8

One of the many things Mama has given up while trying to establish a new food culture for our family is great big hams. Instead, she now cooks half salmons.

When I was growing up, Martha Stamps would help us with our party cooking from time to time. Martha owned a restaurant, had a catering business, and wrote cookbooks. I grew up eating at Martha's at the Plantation and I grew up nibbling on Martha-made deliciousness in my own home. One of the things she cooked for us most often was roasted salmon.

These days Martha cooks in a church kitchen and is very involved with food justice. Entering the kitchen, you walk through a heavy wooden Gothic-looking door. Just outside is a fantastic garden of her creation, with veggies and flowers destined for the table she creates.

One rare cool and dry bright-skied July day, Martha schooled me in the roasting of salmon. When I arrived for the lesson a bouquet of aromatics, from tall lemongrass to feathery dill, was lying on her work table. It smelled great even before we started. The herbs can change with the season or be based on what's available near you.

1 whole fresh salmon fillet (about 3 pounds)

3 tablespoons olive oil

1/2 teaspoon salt

1/2 teaspoon pepper

1/2 teaspoon crushed red pepper flakes

4 stalks lemongrass, halved lengthwise

5 sprigs fresh dill

3 sprigs fresh tarragon

2 lemons, halved

1 Preheat the oven to 425°F.

2 Line a large rimmed baking sheet with parchment paper or aluminum foil, and put the salmon on it. Pour 2 tablespoons of the olive oil over the salmon, then sprinkle the salt, pepper, and red pepper flakes on top. Distribute the lemongrass, dill, and tarragon across the salmon so that they are spaced evenly and nice to look at, too! Pour the last table-spoon of olive oil over the herbs.

3 Roast the salmon until the flesh pulls apart easily and the center is nearly opaque, about 20 minutes. Remember that the fish will keep cooking for a little while even after you take it out of the oven. Squeeze the juice from both lemons over the salmon. Serve hot, or allow to cool and then refrigerate before serving cold.

BREAKFAST
CASSEROLE

SERVES 12

When I first fell in love with breakfast casserole, it was a version that contained full-fat cheddar cheese, fatty pork sausage, whole eggs, and cups of grits. It was decadent and delicious and something that just had to be eaten on Thanksgiving morning. Stripped of much of the fat, this version of breakfast casserole is different, but equally delicious—and quicker to make. Mama has served this to visiting physicians and noted black cardiologists; I serve it at Sunday dinner to musicians trying to get over their hardworking Saturday night. Whomever you're serving, they'll finish it all.

1 teaspoon dried oregano

1 teaspoon crushed red pepper flakes

1 teaspoon garlic powder

1 teaspoon salt

½ tablespoon ground nutmeg

1 pound ground turkey

1 tablespoon olive oil

6 large leeks, white and light green parts, chopped and well rinsed

2 cups cottage cheese

4 ounces (½ cup) fresh goat cheese

4 cups tightly packed chopped fresh spinach

1 quart egg whites (from about 16 large eggs), lightly beaten

1 In a large bowl, mix the oregano, red pepper flakes, garlic powder, salt, and nutmeg. Add the turkey and mix with a spatula or your hands.

2 Slick a large skillet with the olive oil and heat it over medium heat. Add the turkey mixture and cook until the meat is no longer pink, and a meat thermometer reads 165°F, about 7 minutes. Add the leeks and cook for another minute; then add the cottage cheese and goat cheese. Keep cooking and stirring over low heat until the goat cheese just begins to melt.

3 Pour the turkey mixture into a 9 x 13-inch baking dish. Spread the spinach on top, and then pour in the egg whites. Use a spatula to make sure the egg whites are distributed evenly in the dish. Cover with plastic wrap and refrigerate for at least 1 hour, or overnight.

4 Preheat the oven to 350°F.

5 Bake the casserole until a knife stuck into the center comes out clean; about 45 minutes. Serve hot.

GRANDMA'S
CHIA PUDDING

SERVES 16 TO 20

When Langston Hughes named one of his most beloved characters after Grandma, she knew she had arrived at a significant moment of recognition. She was no longer just the mystery of the Harlem Renaissance, no longer just Arna's muse. She was, in some way, Lang's muse, too. Ostensibly, Grandma, the proper poet's wife and matron, wasn't a bit like Hughes's character, Alberta K. Johnson, who had phone bills she couldn't pay and did day work for a white woman—but Grandma loved Alberta K. Johnson, aka Madam, and somewhere beyond the events of their lives they shared a spirit.

During the Great Depression, Grandma cooked and ate so much oatmeal that she decided she would never eat it again when happy days returned. In her ninety-seven years she would travel a far piece from Waycross, Georgia. This recipe continues her journey.

I think of chia seeds as the perfect better-than-oatmeal breakfast for a crowd. Laura Lea Bryant, a good friend of mine and Mama's, created this recipe to feed almost two hundred of Mama's students and their families. This version is scaled down.

Chia puddings are a lot like Grandma—calm and spunky at the same time. They give you energy and keep you moving. Grandma would love the efficiency of this dish. You make it the night before and you wake up to a sophisticated global breakfast that only needs to be pulled out of the refrigerator.

3 quarts unsweetened coconut milk

2 cups white chia seeds

1½ cups maple syrup

2 tablespoons pure vanilla extract

2 teaspoons ground cinnamon

Pour the coconut milk into a large mixing bowl. Add the chia seeds, maple syrup, vanilla, and cinnamon and stir with a whisk until all the ingredients are evenly distributed. Continue stirring the mixture every 2 to 3 minutes for 20 minutes, to prevent clumping, until the pudding is quite thick and difficult to stir. Cover with plastic wrap and refrigerate overnight before serving.

NOTE For a fancy breakfast, or even a dessert, we like to serve chia pudding chilled in small teacups with chopped fresh fruit on top.

Afterword . . .
AND A PRAYER

As we finished the manuscript for this book we found ourselves at the end of one long journey and ready to start another. We began to plan a trip to Alabama. Mama imagined rolling across the Edmund Pettus Bridge blowing kisses and prayers to all the heroes of Bloody Sunday and all the bodies in the Alabama River. I imagined finding our way from the black-top highway to a dirt road, in search of land where Dear's mama, Betty, raised chickens, turkeys, and hogs, and grew beets, turnip greens, collard greens, okra, peppers, watermelons, and yes, those famous Alabama blackberries and dewberries.

Our hope for that trip was that something—maybe some wild blackberry or dewberry bush—would still be growing, and would welcome us back.

By the time you read this book we will have made that trip. In honor of our journey's end we came up with this recipe:

FRUIT PLATE

SERVES 4

Set out your prettiest plate, and conjure up your favorite relatives.

Next, allowing family spirits to pick nature's sweets, arrange on the plate:

Blackberries for Dear in Selma

Plums for Grandma Bontemps's
Geneva Circle Garden

Apricots for Mama

A raw Asian pear for Baby Girl

Nibble at daybreak. Wash down with hot rooibos tea.

We will spend the rest of our lives putting fruits and vegetables onto our plates, and inviting fruits and vegetables onto the plates of others. As well as some lean meat. And some whole grains. Ancient and modern. That's how we embrace the farm that neither Dear nor Grandma could.

We are not new to the farm. In 1977 Mama wrote her get-into-college essay about the two-hundred-plant strawberry patch that she planted while in high school. Working largely alone, she set, watered, and hand-weeded the patch across two summers. She also helped grow corn and asparagus. Mama was so fascinated by asparagus farming that my father, the State Department officer, gave her a golden asparagus pin as a promise that one day they would live long enough in the same place to grow asparagus for the table in their backyard. Mama knew from hard work that that took three years.

But the future of food does not lie in the rural farm of the past. We're excited about urban gardens. How could we not be? Detroit, the town where Mama was born, now boasts more than two thousand gardens and has become the center of the urban gardening movement in the United States. It's also home to several black-owned food co-ops.

So, after Alabama, we will go to Detroit, purchase some of those beautiful Motown greens, wash them seven times, and then whirl them up to make a fine raw juice. We would like to see juicers replace deep-fryers in black family kitchens.

This cookbook is a thank-you note, an act of gratitude for every home that's been created, every table that's been set, every plate that's been filled by a black woman trying to feed her family. And it's a thanks to my mother for making the decision to be the last fat black woman in our family while honoring all the great and grand women who go before us.

And it is an invitation to all families to return to the home kitchen and the home table, to create handmade and healthy dishes at home.

Soul Food Love is about amping up the life-sustaining power of the twenty-first-century black American kitchen by getting back to our strongest roots—and boldly growing new shoots.

GRACE
Bless this table,
and make us truly thankful,
for the food which we are about to receive
prepared in the spirit
of those we love who've come before us
those we love who are now with us
and those we love who are yet to come
that this table might provide
for the comfort of our souls
the hopes of our futures
and the nourishment of our bodies.

Acknowledgments

Without our editor, Rica Allannic; our agent, Amy Williams; and our photographer, Penny De Los Santos, this book would not be. We love Rica, adore Amy, and worship Penny.

Random House has been very, very good to us. We would like to thank Aaron Wehner, Pam Krauss, Doris Cooper, La Tricia Watford, Jane Treuhaft, Michael Nagin, Jess Morphew, Jim Massey, Sigi Nacson, Kim Tyner, Anna Mintz, Carly Gorga, and Sara Katz. The Clarkson Potter team is genius.

Susan Spungen was our food stylist, but more than that she was an inspiration, a provocation, and a pure pleasure to have in Nashville. We have loved her work for a very long time, and it was a dream come real to work with her. Sarah Cave, our prop stylist, reimagined with us the aesthetics of the new soul table.

Special thanks to the stunningly beautiful and talented Natalie Chanin of Alabama Chanin, who dressed Caroline in clothes that shared the aesthetic of our kitchens. We think our food tastes like Natalie Chanin's clothes look. We also want to thank Sherita Leslie, our makeup artist. She lives and celebrates brown beauty.

Mayme Gretsch tested all the recipes and provided useful feedback. We thank her. We also want to thank Josh Habiger, a dear friend and innovative chef, for cheering us on and providing tangible advice. Tandy Wilson has fed us through the writing of all our books and contributed a recipe to this volume. We owe Tandy many thanks for bites of joy and inspiration. Laura Lea Bryant contributed a recipe while helping Alice develop a healthy food curriculum for first-year students at Vanderbilt. Randy Rayburn and Margot McCormack have fed us and inspired us for a good long while. Michael Ryan King, a dear friend with an eye for beautiful objects, helped us with the Nashville prop styling. Dr. David Kirk Barton provided useful psychological insights into the intersections of race, trauma, and table. We thank him for that, and for reminding us to celebrate sesame seeds.

We thank Godmommy Lea, Leatrice McKissack, for being the best home cook still walking this earth that we know. And she does it while juggling, at various times (and sometimes at the same time), the duties of being the president of a national architectural firm, a wife, a mother, a healthy person, and a beautiful black woman.

John Egerton was with us when we started this book. He had eaten at Grandma's, Nana's, Mama's, and Baby Girl's tables, only missing Dear's. The family relationship goes back a half century. His belief that this was an important project made us bold to get working. He blessed this book by eating many of the recipes at our table. We miss him much.

John T. Edge is a taste-sustainer and writer whom we're proud to call friend. An early discussion with John T. on the porch of Snackbar about the cooking and reading habits of Joan Williams helped define the approach we would take with our material. We also want to thank the entire gang at the Southern Foodways Alliance for being profoundly welcoming.

Many local artisan food providers supported this project—the Nelson Brothers, Andy and Charles at Belle Meade Bourbon, and their divine cousin Carrington Nelson Fox, who provided eggs from her urban chickens. Scott Witherow of Olive and Sinclair Chocolate Co. Porter Road Butcher. Green Door Gourmet. Thank you for standing with us. Across the country we want to thank Bob Polovneff at Ocean Mist Farms in California for the amazing artichokes.

We want to send warm thanks to East Ivy Mansion for hosting our New York photo team when they were in Nashville.

As we have become increasingly involved with health issues facing black American women, we have been supported by recognition from Leslie Curtis at the National Institutes of Health and her very able associate Tawanna Campbell. We will be forever indebted to Ruth Ann Harnisch and the Harnisch Foundation for support of our efforts to attack the obesity epidemic using nontraditional weapons. We are also indebted to Mary Bufwack at United Neighborhood Health Services and the Memorial Foundation led by J. D. Elliott for working with us to provide innovative solutions to intractable problems. We are grateful to Vanderbilt's Curb Center for providing early and ongoing support for our effort to explore the uses of art, including the culinary arts, in the service of health.

David Feinberg got us back to loving farms by inviting us to spend long weeks in the countryside in Chilmark on Martha's Vineyard.

Tracy Sharpley-Whiting supported the development of the course "Soul Food in Text, as Text" at Vanderbilt University and edited the first scholarly volume that included work by both of us. We thank her for her brilliance and her friendship. And we thank Adam Platt for his.

We owe a huge debt of gratitude to Caroline's Mississippi universe, the universe where this new soul kitchen really came to life. Adrienne Gispen and Everett Bexley were valiant ever-ready taste-testers and cohosts. Ruthie Collins's friendship, food thoughts, and tough love helped Caroline to survive and then thrive in her first year. Her first graders at James C. Rosser Elementary and her ninth graders at Ruleville Central High School taught her to love Mississippi. Her classmates and mentors—with particular thanks to Beth Ann Fennely, Ivo Kamps, and Derrick Harriel—at the University of Mississippi helped support her in bringing this book to life.

A special thanks to Ruby Amanfu, Ben Cameron, Gabe Fotsing, Amanda Little, Carter Little, Lissa Smith, Edwin Williamson, and our very own David Steele Ewing for being our costars in the Nashville photo shoot.

And near last, but not least, we thank Hatch Show Print. The illustrations in this book were created by the brilliant Bethany Taylor, whom we first met at Hatch. For almost two decades we have worked with master artist-designer Jim Sherraden to create invitations for our yearly Christmas party using hand-carved wood and linoleum blocks created by artists working for Hatch during the 135 years the legendary print shop has been in existence. These days Celene Aubry manages Hatch. Without Celene's help we would not have been able to share with you the images that have meant so much to us.

Mimi Oka more than doubled the size of Caroline's cookbook collection by adding another two thousand volumes; for this and so much more we are grateful to Mimi and her dear husband, Jun Makihara, who has treated us to more amazing meals than we can count—we love them both as chosen family.

In many, many ways this book is a love letter to the family we did not choose—to those with whom we share blood. We thank all the relatives living and dead who shared their stories with us. And we thank all who come to share in them.

Index

Note: Page references in *italics* indicate photographs.